PATTERNS OF INCLUSION

It is widely presumed that digitalisation, automation and artificial intelligence (AI) shape the future of work; yet, gender is rarely considered in those debates. This ground-breaking book, written by a leading thinker on gender, inclusion and organisations, is based on in-depth research to show which patterns of gender and digitalisation emerge. By weaving these different patterns together, is it possible to understand the dynamic and complex ways gender and digitalisation intertwine in the work context?

The book highlights how futures of work are imagined between automation and augmentation: it shows which tasks are expected to be done by machines, and where humans are expected to have a competitive advantage. The book showcases how algorithmic bias is constructed as ultimately fixable, and analyses in/visibilities in AI production processes. Above all, the book shows how patterns relating to gender and inclusion are shaped and could be reshaped.

This innovative book provides a stimulating and provocative read for those who are interested in how automation and AI shape the future of work in regard to gender and what this means for inclusion.

Elisabeth Kelan is Professor of Leadership and Organisation at Essex Business School, University of Essex, United Kingdom. Kelan is an expert on gender and digitalisation, women's leadership, men as change agents for gender equality, generations at work, and diversity and inclusion.

"A ground-breaking book that fills a critical gap by providing a much-needed thorough analysis through a gender lens of perspectives on the potential impacts of automation and AI on the future of work. It enables us to imagine more inclusive and equitable scenarios that better equip us to forge a fairer digital future for all."

Ursula Wynhoven, *Director and Representative to the United Nations, International Telecommunication Union*

"An important work that provides unique, timely and exceptional insights into the digitalisation of gender. Through rigorous research, Elisabeth Kelan illuminates the gendered values, decisions and biases that shape digitalisation, automation and artificial intelligence systems, and why they must be grounded in equity and inclusion."

Melissa Suzanne Fisher, *New York University Institute for Public Knowledge and School of Professional Studies*

PATTERNS OF INCLUSION

How Gender Matters for Automation, Artificial Intelligence and the Future of Work

Elisabeth Kelan

Routledge
Taylor & Francis Group

LONDON AND NEW YORK

Designed cover image: Getty Images/anna

First published 2025
by Routledge
4 Park Square, Milton Park, Abingdon, Oxon OX14 4RN

and by Routledge
605 Third Avenue, New York, NY 10158

Routledge is an imprint of the Taylor & Francis Group, an informa business

This book is based on a Leverhulme Trust Major Research Fellowship [MRF-2019-069]
and reports findings from a project funded by the British Academy [SRG20\200195].
This publication was supported by the University of Essex's Open Access Fund.

Data Availability Statement
Due to the nature of this research, participants of this book did not agree for their
data to be shared publicly, so supporting data is not available.

British Library Cataloguing-in-Publication Data
A catalogue record for this book is available from the British Library

ISBN: 9781032731728 (hbk)
ISBN: 9781032669892 (pbk)
ISBN: 9781003427100 (ebk)

DOI: 10.4324/9781003427100

Typeset in Joanna
by Newgen

To Michael, who always encourages me to be curious about technologies.

CONTENTS

PREFACE

I have been fascinated with discourses on the future of work in relation to gender and technology for a long time. In fact, it was the topic of my Master's dissertation and inspired my subsequent PhD. After working on a range of other issues in the field of gender, diversity and inclusion, I returned to questions of the future of work, gender and technology in late 2018. The future of work in relation to technology was again a big topic at the time and questions of if machines are taking people's jobs made regular headlines. Yet how gender features in the technology-driven future of work was rarely discussed. This was surprising because gender and technology was certainly a topic that was of interest to many more academics. When I first studied gender and technology in the early 2000s, gender and technology was somewhat regarded as niche within gender studies. By 2018, many more scholars engaged in questions of gender and digital technologies, although fewer focused on work.

As a consequence, I identified a research agenda for gender, digitisation and the future of work. This research agenda contained what I saw as important yet understudied aspects in relation to gender, technology and the future of work. I wrote this up as a research proposal that I submitted for a Leverhulme Trust Major Research Fellowship in early 2019. These fellowships are unique in that they afford academics the ability to focus on a distinct piece of research while being relieved of normal teaching and administrative duties. These fellowships are a bit like gold dust: desirable

and hard to obtain. Success rates for funding are low and I fully expected
for the research proposal to be rejected, but much to my delight, I found
out that I had been selected for the fellowship.

When the fellowship started in autumn 2020, the world had changed
dramatically. In early 2020, I was part of the senior management team at
Essex Business School. I remember sitting in meetings where our marketing
colleagues talked about the fact that the rate of students from China who
had accepted places on our degree programmes had gone down. The
rationale offered was a lockdown in a local province. The expectation
was that this was a regional event. By the time I was scheduled to fly out
to Tokyo in March 2020 to take up a visiting professorship there, it had
become clear that the world was at the start of a pandemic. Needless to
say, I did not travel to Japan. The World Health Organization declared an
end to the Public Health Emergency of International Concern (PHEIC) on
5 May 2023 (World Health Organization, 2023). By that time, most of the
fellowship period had taken place during a pandemic. The pandemic shaped
the research substantially. This book is not about gender and the pandemic,
which other research has covered in various shapes and formats (Carli,
2020; Fisher & Ryan, 2021; Flor et al., 2022; Mavin & Yusupova, 2020; Gill
& Orgad, 2022), yet the research is deeply intertwined with the Covid-19
pandemic in relation to gender, digitalisation and the future of work. The
pandemic meant that many traditional ways of working and engaging with
technology were reshaped. It also meant that how I conducted the research
became much more digital and virtual than I had originally envisaged.

Many of the technological changes we observed in everyday work were
probably accelerated by the pandemic. This period of time also indicates
how intertwined gender and technology are, which makes this dynamic
hard to predict. Take, for instance, a standard example for gender and technology: it is presumed that women cashiers in supermarkets are being
replaced by self-check-out machines. When my local supermarket installed
machines for self-check-out, the supermarket nevertheless decided to have
one of the cashiers stand next to the machines. They are presumably there
to help customers struggling to operate the machines but possibly also have
a monitoring function to ensure that customers are honest when scanning
their products. In this local supermarket, there is one cashier who had the
habit of being rather rude with customers and regularly telling them off
for wrong behaviour such as placing their shopping basket in the wrong

location. She had a reputation for being grumpy. When I used the self-check-out, I was anxious when I saw that this cashier was in charge of these machines. I wondered what she would tell me and the other customers if we were unable to operate the machines. However, much to my surprise, this cashier was friendly and most helpful to customers. A complete transformation of the behaviour she had displayed earlier. The second time I encountered her supervising the self-check-out, I was paying for my groceries. The basket next to me was empty and I had planned to pick it up after the payment had gone through. I suddenly noticed how she came next to me and picked up the basket, telling me that she will take care of the basket for me. Rather than telling me off for not putting the basket away quickly enough, she offered to do this for me. It could be that the boredom and monotony of checking out people's groceries is contributing to her being in a bad mood. She might see self-check-out machines as a job enrichment. Maybe she sees supervising machines or rather supervising customers using machines as a way to secure her job into the future. These are of course speculations. However, it shows that dynamics around gender and digitalisation are hard to predict.

Yet such cashier jobs alongside those of many delivery riders might still disappear if autonomous robots deliver groceries to our homes. From my desk at home, I could observe how humans interact with these autonomous delivery robots that were navigating the pavement outside of my window. These robots are regularly getting stuck in an evasion bay and then struggle to climb back up onto the pavement. Over the years, I have not only observed that these robots do not learn how to navigate the evasion bay but I also noticed that many people would stop and help the robot. People would get off their bikes and out of their cars to lift the robot back to the pavement, often talking to them ('here you go, mate'). There are of course the occasional pedestrians who attempt to obstruct the robots as well. In those cases, the robots talk to these humans to say things like 'I am late, please let me pass'. Such interactions and the anthropomorphising entailed in them will provide rich material for researchers for years to come.

It is also important to remember that the infrastructures that are being created around digitalisation will exist for years to come. If I think for instance about the infrastructure that is provided in my current house, not much has changed for a long time: electricity, water and sewage and a copper telephone line. Once in place, these infrastructures are hard to change. As such, it is important to reflect on what infrastructures we put in place for digitalisation because they too might last a long time. However, things change. I live in a modern, state-of-the-art eco-house in the UK. It is only 12 years old. Yet even 12 years ago, no provision was made that infrastructures might need to change. The recent arrival of fibre internet in my area is a case in point. The road was dug up and new cables were laid. Since the copper lines will be retired soon, to ensure that the house retains a connection to the internet, those cables eventually had to be connected to the house, requiring even more digging and drilling. Even in a modern house, there were no provisions for the fact that infrastructures might need to change. As such, it seems wise to plan for the unexpected and retain some slack in the digital infrastructures that are being created.

This book presents a snapshot of how gender and digitalisation can be theorised in a world where work, alongside many other aspects of life, appear to be in flux. The book also suggests that gender and digitalisation are shaped by society while also shaping society. The dynamic interplay between gender and digitalisation is often unfolding in predictable patterns, but as the book shows, there might be opportunities to change those patterns. While some of those patterns entrench inequalities, patterns might also create opportunities for inclusion.

ACKNOWLEDGEMENTS

This book would not have been possible without the generous support provided by a Leverhulme Trust Major Research Fellowship [MRF-2019-069]. The fellowship has enabled me to focus on completing the underlying research for this book. It also allowed me to write the book itself. I am extremely grateful for this support.

The material I report on in Chapter 5 was collected with funding from the British Academy's Small Grant programme [SRG20\200195], which I am grateful for.

The digital publication in Open Access format was supported by the University of Essex's Open Access fund.

I would like to acknowledge the research support from Jules Allen, Claire Durrant and Jarek Kriukow during different parts of the research process. Thanks also to Lisa Woodford and Trixie Gadd for proofreading parts of this manuscript.

I am extremely grateful to Rosalind Gill and Judy Wajcman for inspiring so much of my research and for their unwavering support for my work. Thanks also to all colleagues who have provided feedback and comments on the research in formal and informal settings. This book profited immensely from such discussions.

It has been fantastic to work with the team at Routledge on this publication. In particular, Rebecca Marsh not only believed in this book but also provided invaluable feedback.

Essex Business School has provided an intellectually stimulating home during the research for and writing of the book. I could not have wished for more supportive colleagues.

I am deeply grateful to my family for giving me the time and space to write this book.

Some of the material covered in this book has been published in academic journals with Wiley:

Kelan, E. K. (2024). Algorithmic inclusion: Shaping the predictive algorithms of artificial intelligence in hiring. *Human Resource Management Journal*, online early.

Kelan, E. K. (2023). Automation anxiety and augmentation aspiration: Subtexts of the future of work. *British Journal of Management*, 34(4), 2057–2074.

Finally, I am extremely grateful to those individuals who kindly shared their experiences and reflections with me during the interviews. I would also like to thank those who have provided access to technology which I could explore for this research. This book would not have been possible without this support.

1

INTRODUCTION

HUMAN-LIKE

Introduction

The future of work and digitalisation is a topic that is dominating discussions in the media and in many organisations. While the future of work is regularly invoked, it has been suggested that the term 'future of work' is polysemous with various meanings attached to it. While how gender matters in these transformation processes is regularly ignored, how gender is relevant for digitalisation at work takes centre stage in this book. Based on detailed empirical research, I suggest in this book that we need to look at patterns around gender and technology that emerge in different settings. However, only by weaving together these different patterns is it possible to understand the dynamic and complex ways in which gender and digitalisation in the work context are intertwined. This introductory chapter discusses why focusing on how the future of work is imagined is central for which futures are being made possible and impossible. I also suggest that technologies are often imbued with magical and mythical qualities in everyday conversations. I then turn to discussing how the gender–technology dynamic is understood before explaining the underlying research for and the structure of this book. The book argues that we need to understand the dynamics between gender and digitalisation in the work context to create more equitable futures.

DOI: 10.4324/9781003427100-1

Imagining Futures of Work and Human-Like Intelligence

The future of work is a topic that enjoys a constant interest – multiple reports and books are authored every year that trace the question of what the future of work might hold. Wajcman (2017) observes that predicting the future of work has become 'big business'. This extends to conferences on that topic. She finds that such conferences follow a familiar and pre-dictable pattern: technologists marvel at the latest technological progress, economists paint a concerning picture of the future of jobs and futurists predict the next trends (Wajcman, 2017). The term 'future of work' in itself has been described as a 'floating signifier' to which various meanings are attached by different groups (Schlogl et al., 2021). A common feature for discussions on the future of work is that they play with the dichotomy between utopia and dystopia (Schlogl et al., 2021; Howcroft & Taylor, 2023).

One could argue that how the future is imagined has limited consequences because most of such predictions tend to be wrong anyway. However, it would be a mistake to dismiss these predictions of the future as irrelevant or meaningless. Such visions for the future have profound consequences for societies because they create ideas of what might be possible (Urry, 2016). They also create realities (Schlogl et al., 2021). Urry (2016) warns against seeing futures simply based on a predetermined path of develop-ment of technologies or as seeing futures as completely open and empty. How futures are imagined, for instance, in discourses on the future of work, shapes what might or might not be possible.

Science fiction can provide a blueprint of how potential desirable or undesirable futures are imagined, which then influences what is seen as possible (Jasanoff, 2015). Instead, Jasanoff (2015) follows the idea that society and technology are co-constructed. Such a co-construction becomes manifest in sociotechnical imaginaries (Jasanoff, 2015). Sociotechnical imaginaries are 'collectively held, institutionally stabilized, and publicly performed visions of desirable futures, animated by shared understandings of forms of social life and social order attainable through, and supportive of, advances in science and technology' (Jasanoff, 2015, p. 4). In other words, sociotechnical imaginaries are a way to analyse how individuals are engaging in collective practices when imaging the future. Diverging sociotechnical imaginaries can coexist and shape one another, and are evaluated and debated through societal discourses. Even though most sociotechnical imaginaries are ultimately interested in shaping futures that are desirable, they often do so by outlining scenarios that ought to be avoided; the tension between a desirable utopia and an undesirable dystopia is actively used in sociotechnical imaginaries (Jasanoff, 2015).

Much of the literature on the future of work attempts to warn of undesirable dystopias, particularly through job losses associated with technologies. Many of the widely cited reports on the future of work engage in predictions on what the future of work might entail and how many jobs are going to be lost due to automation that is driven by technologies (Manyika, Chui, & Miremadi, 2017; Hawksworth, Berriman, & Goel, 2018; Organisation for Economic Cooperation and Development [OECD], 2016; World Economic Forum, 2020; Balliester & Elsheikhi, 2018; Hatzius et al., 2023). It is also common to contextualise current changes in regard to different industrial revolutions. Schwab (2018) suggests that the First Industrial Revolution was marked by mechanisation of the textile industry in Britain; the second was associated with electricity, the telephone and the automobile; the third was related to changes in digital computing in the 1950s; and the fourth is marked by a range of new technologies, including artificial intelligence (AI), distributed ledgers (blockchain), advanced materials and virtual and augmented realities. Schwab (2018) predicts that exponential growth in these new technologies will lead to rapid change, and that automation may accelerate job losses. In contrast, McAfee and Brynjolfsson (2014) coined the term 'second machine age'. The first machine age is equated with the Industrial Revolution when machines improved human labour; the second machine age is said to have begun in the mid-1990s with digitalisation and is characterised by machines not simply following rules but solving problems on their own. Thus, machines now perform cognitive tasks previously reserved for humans. This leads to fears that humans are replaced by machines.

Fears of humans being replaced by machines are of course not new. For instance, during what Schwab (2018) would call the First Industrial Revolution, the relationship between machines and humans was redrawn and a common perception was that machines are going to replace physical power that people had exerted before (Standage, 2002). However, the arrival of the Mechanical Turk, the 18th-century life-size chess-playing automaton (see Chapter 5), challenged this idea, because the Mechanical Turk seemed to outperform humans mentally (Standage, 2002). Although what appeared magical to audiences at the time turned out to be a hoax, the possibility that machines could outdo humans mentally was certainly part of the fascination with the Mechanical Turk.

This blurring of what constitutes human and what constitutes machine intelligence is also visible in how Joseph Weizenbaum's chatbot ELIZA was received. ELIZA was a natural language processing computer programme developed by Joseph Weizenbaum in the 1960s to explore how humans and machines communicate. The name ELIZA was chosen as a reference to Eliza Doolittle in George Bernard Shaw's play *Pygmalion* (Natale, 2019; Dillon, 2020). This choice of name carries strong gender and class connotations (Dillon, 2020). Weizenbaum's aim with ELIZA was to show humans that AI is an illusion (Natale, 2019). However, Weizenbaum was shocked by the fact that rather than recognising the difference between human intelligence and AI, humans engaged emotionally with the machine and anthropomorphised it (Treusch, 2017). In other words, users perceived ELIZA's answers as human-like. Even when users, such as Weizenbaum's secretary, knew that ELIZA was not engaging on an emotional level, they ascribed emotional competence to the chatbot (Dillon, 2020; Treusch, 2017; Rhee, 2023). The 'ELIZA effect' describes how humans presume more intelligence in a machine than really exists (Hofstadter, 1995; Dillon, 2020). While we return to the gendering of current virtual personal assistants (VPAs) (see Chapter 5), Dillon observes that 'when a human being is conversing with a VPA, the brain is processing that conversation as it would a conversation with another human being. The Eliza (sic) effect is here embedded in the neural response to the voice' (Dillon, 2020, p. 11). Humans thus engage with machine-generated voices in the same way as with human voices. This supports the illusions of AI as human-like intelligence rather than exposing it as an illusion, as Weizenbaum had hoped. When ChatGPT reached the mainstream in late 2022, many commentators similarly marvelled at the human-like answers the chatbot was able to provide (Hatzius et al., 2023). It was exactly this human-likeness that promoted concerns that human mental capacities could be replaced with machines (Hatzius et al., 2023). This in many ways echoes Weizenbaum's own concern about AI, which he wanted to expose with ELIZA (Treusch, 2017), but also the wider concerns that humans will be replaced by machines.

Although predictions about humans being replaced by machines appear as dystopian and are usually followed with calls for a universal basic income, there are also sociotechnical imaginaries that are utopian and as such more hopeful. Here, utopias are imagined as desirable, where humans can focus on specific tasks: those where humans have a competitive advantage or where they collaborate with machines (Hatzius et al., 2023; Daugherty & Wilson, 2018). It is argued that these technologies also mean that new jobs emerge, and while some jobs disappear, new ones will be created (Hatzius et al., 2023). Existing jobs might also be enhanced by technologies through new human–machine collaboration (Daugherty & Wilson, 2018). These utopian discourses are closely associated with what has been called augmentation, where humans and machines augment each other's skills (Raisch & Krakowski, 2021). While automation is largely associated with dystopian ideas of jobs being replaced by machines, augmentation represents the utopian idea that humans can either focus on activities where they outperform machines or collaborate with machines.

Although automation and augmentation are often presented as opposing, most workplaces will experience both automation and augmentation to different degrees. This in itself is not a new phenomenon. When Sennett (1998) returned to a bakery that he had visited many years before, he noticed how the process of baking bread has been computerised; the bakers no longer made psychical contact with the ingredients and monitored the bread-making process via screens. Sennett (1998) argues that this leads to a deskilling and alienation of bakers with no hands-on knowledge of how to produce bread. Work has become what Sennett (1998) calls 'illegible' to the bakers. This pre-empted Sennett's (2008) later argument that craftwork is a way through which people comprehend their worlds. Of course, many people would argue that the digitalisation of bread making is enhancing bakers' skills – they need to know about technology and how to engage with this technology to achieve optimal results. In fact, Sennett (1998) describes that bakers manipulate the machines if something goes wrong and thus develop additional knowledge, but he still maintains that bakers have lost the ability to bake bread in the traditional sense. As digitalisation changes the skills required for jobs, such arguments suggest that certain skills will no longer be required and will be lost because people do not invest time in honing them. This means that while some jobs will be automated and might disappear over time, digitalisation will also change the skills required to do existing jobs.

There is also an important change to which jobs are expected to disappear. While in the past, blue-collar work was presumed to be automated, it has more recently been suggested that the focus of job replacement due to automation has moved to white-collar professional jobs (cf. Wajcman, 2017; Howcroft & Rubery, 2019; Cave, 2020). This marks a shift from machines replacing physical human power, to machines threatening to replace human minds. They emulate human intelligence. While some jobs might be replaced due to technologies in professional services, it can also be expected that the tasks professionals do will change. Digitalisation will affect temporalities in those professions. For instance, when spreadsheets were first introduced, accountants were able to complete tasks quicker due to automation, but clients also started to expect a quicker turnaround and also more analytical insight (O'Connor, 2023). Similarly, the introduction of new communication tools like online videoconferencing via Zoom and shared calendars has led to more work rather than less with ever-decreasing increments of time immediately filled by demands, leading to the conclusion that 'white-collar work always seems to expand to fill the time available' (O'Connor, 2023). This chimes with research that has shown that the idea that digital calendars optimise one's time is a false belief because such technologies are not giving individuals more time (Wajcman, 2019). Instead, digital technologies contribute to an acceleration of everyday life (Wajcman, 2015). Similarly, technologies that are expected to be time saving often do not deliver on the expected effects. Cowan (1983) shows how household technologies, which should save effort and time on household tasks, meant that mothers and wives increasingly took on household activities that had previously been completed by fathers, husbands, children and servants. As such, household technologies did contribute to an intensification of what mothers are expected to do without freeing up time (Cowan, 1983).

Talking about household technologies also draws attention to how the future of work is commonly framed: most discussions on the future of work focus on paid work rather than unpaid work (Lehdonvirta et al., 2023). Work done in the home such as caring for children or elderly relatives, preparing meals or writing birthday cards is virtually never discussed in relation to the future of work. Feminists have long made the argument that work should encompass work done in the household (Oakley, 2018; England & Lawson, 2005). This can entail unpaid and paid care work where a specific focus in regard to unpaid work is on how this work is often racialised (Ehrenreich & Hochschild, 2003; Gutiérrez-Rodríguez, 2014). Unpaid work at home is also experiencing digitalisation, offering the opportunity to explore what and how automation and augmentation happen and interact with gender (Strengers & Kennedy, 2020; Lehdonvirta et al., 2023).

While it has to be acknowledged that the definition of work employed in discussions of the future of work is narrow and that this is problematic in itself, in this book, I have decided to focus on how such specific perspectives of the world have consequences for how the future of work is imagined. I argue for considering the complex interplay of intersectional inequalities, which is discussed more fully later. Such an analysis allows for questioning what specific views of the world allow us to see and what they obscure. The acknowledgement that work largely focuses on paid work is a necessary but not sufficient analytical tool to make the dynamic interplay of intersectional inequalities visible. The book therefore focuses on work as paid work and acknowledges that such a framing of work is exclusionary because it excludes unpaid care work. However, how the future of (paid) work is imagined is in itself a subject worthy of study because in these sociotechnical imaginaries, patterns of inclusion and exclusion might be perpetuated or challenged.

The Magic of Human-Like Technology

In everyday conversations, terms used to describe current technologies such as digitalisation, AI and algorithms have often a mythical and magical quality to them. Finn (2017) suggests that people have developed a strong belief in algorithms that is faith-like; with little understanding how such technologies operate, Finn (2017) suggests that people believe in them. Finn (2017) argues that machines occupy similar spaces to magical and mythical thinking in primitive societies. Building on Malinowski's influential work, Finn (2017) suggests that technology takes the place of rituals and beliefs in modern societies. Finn (2017) proposes that engaging in rituals such as summoning a ride via Uber fulfils the same function as rituals in primitive societies: it helps humans to deal with danger and uncertainty. In many everyday conversations, terms like algorithm take on a mythical and magical status where these terms are used without fully understanding what they entail and how these technologies work. This mythical and magical nature of terms like algorithms and AI can be exposed by looking at definitions of those terms, which to most individuals working outside a narrow academic field will appear as abstract. However, in order to weaken the mythical and magical power of these terms, it is important to develop an understanding of what these terms refer to without getting lost in the technical definitions of these terms.

A first term one hears regularly is digitalisation. Digitalisation differs first of all from digitisation. Digitisation entails a move from analogue to digital (Oxford English Dictionary, 2023d). For instance, it might be decided to scan all paper records to create a digital replica, which is digitisation. In regard to hiring, it was long common to conduct pen-and-paper psychometric tests, and if the same test is simply offered via a computer, this would also be digitisation. Essential for digitisation is that a digital replica of an object is created. As such, if a train company decides to create digital twins to test, for example, how different rolling stock performs on tracks, this is a form of digitisation. Digitalisation by contrast is a broader concept and refers to the adoption of technology by an organisation, country or industry (Oxford English Dictionary, 2023c). For example, if one transfers a pen-and-paper psychometric test to an online version without any changes, then the delivery of the test changes but the test itself does not change. However, if one uses AI to predict the best candidate for a job, the process itself changes. This is what is commonly meant with digitalisation. Digitalisation is thus a term that describes how processes themselves change due to the application of a digital technology. Digitalisation is also often referred to as digital transformation. Digitalisation itself is a broad term that can entail a myriad of other terms and technologies.

One way in which processes change through digitalisation is automation. Automation means that a process that was previously done by a human is done by a machine, or in other words, '[t]he action or process of introducing automatic equipment or devices into a manufacturing or other process or facility; (also) the fact of making something (as a system, device, etc.) automatic' (Oxford English Dictionary, 2023b). While some automation might use AI, not all automation will necessarily use AI. An example of automation is the car factory: traditionally, humans would have assembled a car but now robots do the same job. This is often contrasted with augmentation, where humans and machines collaborate and augment each other's skills (Raisch & Krakowski, 2021).

One technology that is central for digitalisation is AI. The OECD has defined an AI system as 'a machine-based system that can, for a given set of human-defined objectives, make predictions, recommendations, or decisions influencing real or virtual environments. AI systems are designed to operate with varying levels of autonomy' (OECD, 2019). The European Union defines an AI system in similar terms as

> a machine-based system that is designed to operate with varying levels of autonomy and that may exhibit adaptiveness after deployment, and that, for explicit or implicit objectives, infers, from the input it receives, how to generate outputs such as predictions, content, recommendations, or decisions that can influence physical or virtual environments.'
>
> (European Parliament, 2024, p. 165)

Another definition of AI is that of AI as 'intelligent agents' that perceive their environment and perform actions (Russell & Norvig, 2021). Intelligence here means that a machine appears to display human-like intelligence (Russell & Norvig, 2021).

Much of what is commonly called AI is technically machine learning. Machine learning is a subset of AI. Machine learning means that 'a computer observes some data, builds a model based on the data, and uses the model as both a hypothesis about the world and a piece of software that can solve problems' (Russell & Norvig, 2021, p. 669). Data is central in the machine learning process; commonly, machine learning involves the machine searching for patterns in the data to develop a model of what the machine perceives as true in this context (Broussard, 2018). This is the training or learning part and the model is then tested with new data to see how accurate predictions are (Broussard, 2018). If we want to define AI, a useful definition entails the ways to analyse, derive learning from and make predictions based on data (Kelan, 2024). Based on this definition, we can see that data is central for AI. We see that expressed often in the form of Big Data, which is then analysed, learned from and used as the basis for making predictions. Many writers on the future of work therefore liken data to the 'new oil' (De Cremer, 2020; Frey, 2019; Schwab, 2018) to indicate that data is the new natural resource that has to be mined.

So far, I have not talked about algorithms, which have taken on a particular mythical and magical meaning in everyday perceptions. The term 'algorithm' traces back to Muḥammad ibn Mūsā al-Khwārizmī, a mathematician living in the 9th-century CE in Persia who lent his name to both algorithm and algebra (Finn, 2017). Algorithms are sequences of instructions that have a specific purpose such as solving a problem (Kearns & Roth, 2019). Algorithms perform specific tasks by using input values and, by following a predefined sequence of actions, provide an output. Broussard (2018) describes an algorithm as a mathematical calculation to arrive at a result, which is not unlike a cooking recipe where following specific steps leads to a dish. Most computer programming involves code that contains algorithms that tell the computer which steps to follow to achieve a result. As alluded to before, in fields like machine learning, an algorithm commonly describes a set of instructions provided to a computer to learn from data (Lum & Chowdhury, 2021). The result of this learning process is often called a model (Lum & Chowdhury, 2021). A model is a representation of what the machine has learned from data or what reality it perceives to be true.

Algorithms are often associated with programmers. Traditionally, a programmer would code, for instance, by using various algorithms that tell a machine what actions to perform in a sequence. When I conducted research for my PhD, I observed the work of programmers (Kelan, 2009). For me, the code initially appeared as nonsensical text, but I swiftly discovered – thanks to patient explanations by the programmers – that programming was a language to communicate with a machine to perform actions and the individual segments of the code started to make sense to me. The programmers would write careful documentation explaining the functioning of the segments of code to allow others to repair the code later on if the need arose. Before, I might have perceived the process of logging into a bank account as magical, but after observing the programmers who programmed exactly these steps, I realised at least on a superficial level which steps were needed in programming to allow me to log into my bank account.

However, being able to explain what happens inside a machine is more problematic in machine learning. Here, the designers of such technologies are often far less certain what a machine learned from data or in other words what goes into machine learning models. Domingos (2015) describes this as technology that is building itself or computers that programme themselves. This does not mean that designers of such technologies have no influence at all because they set the parameters for how reality should be represented in technology (Barocas & Selbst, 2016). O'Neil states that '[m]odels are opinions embedded in mathematics' (O'Neil, 2016, p. 21). Instead, it means that even designers of AI often struggle to explain which elements were used to arrive at certain predictions; this contributes to the often-discussed black box effect (Domingos, 2015; Pasquale, 2015; O'Neil, 2016). Machine learning models 'cannot "tell" programmers why they do what they do' (Autor, 2015, p. 26). Programming moved from a well-documented and well-explained process to one where what the computer learns from data might not be transparent to programmers. This lack of transparency of what happens in the black box of machine learning models not only makes it difficult to spot and remedy algorithmic bias, as we will explore in Chapter 4, but it also feeds into the mythical and magical quality that we attribute to such technologies. It is also the reason why explainability and transparency is high on the agenda for policymakers trying to regulate AI (OECD, 2019).

Although technologies often appear as magical, the magic element is often that they emulate humans. Machine learning, for instance, includes deep learning, which uses artificial neural networks to mimic neurones in human or animal brains. In general, many of the technologies are concerned with emulating human functions, such as pattern recognition that is used in speech recognition, chatbots that mimic conversations or expert systems that imitate expert decision-making or computer vision that recognises visual data. Most of such applications of machine learning are built on specialist databases that allow for fairly narrow user requests such as around facial recognition or text classification (Hatzius et al., 2023). Generative AI, which includes ChatGPT, differs in that it is built on general databases such as those sourced from the internet to build large language models that facilitate the use of more advanced natural language processing (Hatzius et al., 2023). When ChatGPT entered mainstream discussions, people commented on how amazed they were that the machine seems to appear original and creative, attributing almost magical qualities to such technologies; users of Twitter (now X) talked about it as a 'mix of software and sorcery' (Roose, 2022). The magic is driven by the fact that generative AI aims to create output that is difficult to distinguish from what a human would create; this is achieved by using a second neural network that checks the output of the first neural network based on the criterion of how human-like the answer is (Hatzius et al., 2023). The human-like nature of answers appears to many people like magic. The magic thus lies in the fact that the output of a machine appears human-like.

So far, I have largely talked about machine learning as an example of AI. However, there are other technologies that are commonly included under the wide umbrella of AI. AI is also often used in relation to robotics, which is concerned with the creation of robots. The term 'robots' can be traced to a play called R.U.R., which stands for Rossum's Universal Robots, by Czech writer Karel Čapek (1920). R.U.R. was written in 1920. Etymologically, a robot goes back to the Czech robota that denotes forced labour or drudgery (for a discussion on drudgery, see also Chapter 3). It was Karel Čapek's brother Josef who suggested this term (Oxford English Dictionary, 2023e). Robots are embodied in that they take a specific shape to complete a task. Robots tend to follow programming, which can include AI if they, for instance, interact with their environment.

Another technology that is regularly mentioned is virtual reality (VR). It is useful to start with the term 'virtual' itself. Virtual as a term goes back to the Latin 'virtue', which originally meant manliness but then stood for power and strength (Chalmers, 2022). Virtual means to stand for or 'as if': a virtual duck is 'as if' a duck (Chalmers, 2022). Although the virtual is commonly distinguished from the real, Chalmers (2022) argues that the virtual is a form of reality. In most cases, VR is accessed through a headset and hand-held controllers. AI is often used in VR to create virtual worlds. Chalmers (2022) describes three conditions to be met for VR: first, VR has to be immersive in that it creates a world around us; second, it needs to be interactive, which entails that there is an interaction between users and objects such as the ability to move virtual objects by moving one's hand; third, it has to be computer generated, which means that the experience is mediated by a computer. If the experience is not fully immersive but virtual objects are projected on a physical world, this is commonly called augmented reality (AR). Increasingly, both VR and AR are offered in the same headsets, which is known as mixed reality or spatial computing (Apple, 2023). Chalmers (2022) uses the example of a virtual kitten and a robot kitten that are both real but not both biological kitten; the kittens are all real but different. Virtual objects exist in computers and they have casual powers that confer realness (Chalmers, 2022). To distinguish these realities,

Chalmers (2022) suggests to use physical/virtual rather than real/virtual. He also suggests developing language that moves from being virtual exclusive to virtual inclusive, and likens this change in language to how marriage has moved towards lesbian, gay, bisexual and transgender (LGBT) inclusion and how man and woman include trans individuals (Chalmers, 2022).

In this section, I have shown that terms like digitalisation, automation and AI encompass a range of different technologies with fluid boundaries. It is common for those technologies to be lumped together and to be treated with little specificity in everyday discussions. Technologists by contrast have developed careful definitions that show how these technologies differ and where they overlap. For the purpose of this book, I want to occupy somewhat a middle ground between the two extremes. It is important to distinguish those technologies to explore how they are shaped and used in different contexts and what consequences arise from that. This book focuses on digitalisation and particularly on automation and AI. I focus on automation in relation to discussions on the future of work, but I also discuss how VR is shaped and used in a work context. Yet in other contexts, I hone in on specific examples from AI and machine learning. Although I discuss in some instances specific technologies, in others, I use digitalisation and AI as umbrella terms to discuss broader concerns. The language I adopt in this book is geared towards fostering an interdisciplinary understanding of what these changes might mean for inclusion. I thus bring terminology used in technology research into conversation with terminology more common for the social sciences and humanities, to allow for a more general understanding of how these changes can be shaped beyond the magic of displaying human-like intelligence.

Gender and Technology as Mutually Constitutive

After discussing how technology is seen in this book, I would now like to turn to discussing the gender–technology relationship. However, to understand the gender–technology relationship, it is first important to elucidate another aspect of technology that has not been discussed thus far. In general discussions on the future of work, there is an underlying tenor of technology determinism. The development and introduction of a new technology leads to specific outcomes for societies and businesses. Such technological determinism is problematic because it ignores that societies shape specific technologies. A commonly deployed example is that of the early development of the refrigerator. Cowan (1999) asks why the gas version of the refrigerator did not succeed and the electric version of the fridge became the dominant technology. Cowan (1999) shows the considerable investment into research and development and associated personnel alongside sophisticated advertising and public relations techniques, together with the vested interest of electric utility companies that funded the development and marketing of electric refrigerators meant that the electric version of the fridge was adopted more widely. The gas version of the refrigerator in contrast did not enjoy the same investment as the electric refrigerator, even though the potential of the gas version of the fridge was regularly lauded as having many advantages. Such an advantage included that the gas version of the refrigerator was silent whereas the electric version had and still has a hum. Additionally, the gas version of the refrigerator was deemed easier to maintain and the operating costs would have been lower at the time because gas was cheaper than electricity. The gas version of the refrigerator failed not because of a technical deficiency as such but because there were social and economic forces at play, which meant that the electric version of the refrigerator became dominant. Larger companies with more resources invested and pushed the electric version of the refrigerator and companies that produced the gas version did not have resources to match. This ultimately meant that the electric version of the refrigerator became dominant.

In order to counter the idea that technological change drives social transformation, MacKenzie and Wajcman (1985, 1999) developed the concept of the social shaping of technology. In fact, the example of the refrigerator influenced the subtitle of the first edited collection that MacKenzie and Wajcman (1985) published: *The Social Shaping of Technology: How the Refrigerator Got Its Hum*. The book also featured Cowan's (1999) chapter on this topic. The second edition of this book (MacKenzie & Wajcman, 1999) developed the concept of the social shaping of technology further, which had since the publication of the original volume developed so much pace that the new edition was more like a follow up than a second edition of the book. Rather than countering the idea of technological determinism with a social determinism, central to the social shaping approach is the notion of that shaping implies materiality; society crystallises in technology and vice versa. This means that the social shapes technology and technology shapes the social. The social shaping of technology approach also acknowledges that technologies often entail path dependency in that existing technologies often shape the next development of such technologies. Another feature of the social shaping of technology is that it acknowledges what Winner (1980) questioned in the famous essay: 'do artefacts have politics'. Winner (1980) used the example of overpasses in New York, which were designed in such a way that buses would not fit. Only those who had access to cars were able to use the overpasses, and by extension, the parks that they led to; this shows an in-built bias in relation to who has access to a car, which was linked to race and class (Winner, 1980). Similarly, the social shaping of technology approach (MacKenzie & Wajcman, 1985, 1999) presumes that technology is not neutral but that it is political.

Wajcman has brought the social shaping of technology approach to bear on gender. In her seminal work, Wajcman (1991, 2004) shows how technology shapes gender and how gender shapes technology. These ideas have been developed further by Faulkner (2001), who provides detail on how the shaping of gender and technology happens. One of the first issues that comes to mind in relation to gender and technology is the scarcity of women among the rows of programmers and designers of new technologies such as in data science (Hicks, 2018; Woodfield, 2000; Twine, 2022; Young et al., 2021, 2023). Faulkner (2001) has theorised that technology is gendered by association: technology work is perceived as something for men, which is why women do not see these jobs as viable career options. As I have shown in my earlier work, how people talk about technology is a way in which people express gender: men talk about technology as toys whereas women talk about technologies as tools (Kelan, 2007). However, Faulkner (2001) also discusses another way in which gender enters technology by design. If technologies are designed, it is not uncommon to conceptualise the user as having certain aptitudes and abilities. A classic example is provided by Hofmann (1999), who traced how the design of office technology was shaped by how the user was imagined. For instance, if one designs an electric version of the typewriter and imagines the user as a female secretary, this influences how the technology itself is designed (Hofmann, 1999). One might here also consider Adam's work (1998) on how rationality is constructed in relation to AI and how men are taken as the norm in much thinking on AI. Wilson (2010) shows that 'chess-like' or 'child-like' foundations of AI are as not oppositional but both imbued with affect; this albeit indirectly also sheds light on how gender and AI are intertwined. If the growing importance of AI is discussed, it is thus central to also explore the gender dynamics entailed in AI (Toupin, 2023).

Distinguishing between gender by association and by design is theoretically useful, but in practice, it is more difficult to distinguish between these two ideas. This is commonly phrased in relation to concerns that the lack of representation of women and other groups in the design of new technologies leads to technologies being biased (see also Chapter 6). While the lack of women among the designers of new technologies could be seen as an exclusion from potentially lucrative careers, the idea that women as designers automatically leads to gender-inclusive design is problematic in itself. First, it ignores the social-shaping dynamics around how technologies are designed, which might, for instance, follow commercial concerns. So even if women have unique insights into the world, which is often expressed as situated knowledge (Haraway, 1991), they might be unable to bring this knowledge to bear on the design process. Second, it presumes that women designers speak for all women. This ignores that a white, middle-class woman might have different views on the world than a Black, working-class woman. Women are positioned differently by intersecting inequalities (Acker, 2006; McCall, 2005; Nash, 2008; Crenshaw, 1989) and whose voices are heard and listened is influenced by complex power dynamics (Spivak, 1988; Mohanty, 1986). Considering gender by association and gender by design is a useful analytical device to understand the social shaping of gender and technology if such analyses consider how women might be positioned differently in relation to technologies.

In order to illustrate reflections that seeing gender and technology as mutually constitutive can lead to, I want to turn to a reading of the Turing Test that is informed by gender. The Turing Test has become emblematic for seeing technology as displaying human-like intelligence. The Turing Test is a thought experiment by Alan Turing, the mathematician and computer scientist, often associated with his work on code breaking at Bletchley Park during the Second World War. Turing's thought experiment (1950) discusses the possibilities around machines being 'intelligent'. In his writing, Turing (1950) suggests that an intelligent machine should be able to perform a game – referred to as the imitation game – that was a popular party game at the time. The core idea of this game is that a human is unable to discern if the answers given originate from a machine or a human (Sutko, 2020).

If a human cannot distinguish the answer from a human and a machine, the machine passes the Turing Test by displaying human-like intelligence.

What is commonly ignored in the popular perception of the Turing Test is the gender dimension of the original Turing Test (Shah & Warwick, 2016; Sutko, 2020; Genova, 1994; Drage & Frabetti, 2023). In order to understand how the Turing Test might relate to gender, it is necessary to explain the imitation game in more detail. The imitation game has three players: a man (A), a woman (B) and an interrogator of either sex[1] (C) (Turing, 1950; Saygin et al., 2000). The aim of the game is for the interrogator (C) to determine who is a woman by asking questions such as about hair length. Both A and B must convince C that they are indeed a woman. The interrogator (C) cannot see either players A and B. The players should not use their voice to communicate because this might give away gender. Instead, they communicate via notes that should ideally be typed up via a teleprinter (Turing, 1950) to not allow conclusion about gender from handwriting.

Turing takes this game a step further where a machine takes the place of A. The most common interpretation of the Turing Test is that C now needs to find out who is the human: A or B (Saygin et al., 2000)? Such an interpretation entails that the aim of the game is no longer to convince C who the woman is but instead who the human is. One might also read this scenario as a way in which A and B attempt to appear as a human woman. Turing himself does not mention that the game has been altered from passing as a woman to passing as a human. Two arguments are used to support this idea. First, in trying to pass as a human woman, neither the man nor the machine has an advantage (Saygin et al., 2000). They both have to impersonate a woman because in the modified version, A is not a man but a machine, whereas B the woman is now B the human. A second argument is that Turing, as a gay man, might have picked gender purposefully to draw attention to gender (Genova, 1994; Hayes & Ford, 1995). While those arguments have some purchase, it seems more likely that Turing in fact did not mean for the game to be about guessing gender, where the human and the machine pass as a woman, but rather about if a machine can convince a human into believing that the machine is indeed human.

However, the idea that gender might be central for the Turing Test provides in itself an interesting thought experiment. If the Turing Test is understood as a man and a machine passing as a woman, this allows for connections with gender theories where gender is often seen as something that is done, achieved and performed (West & Zimmerman, 1987; Butler, 1990).[2] If the Turing Test is seen as a way to pass as a woman, then the man and the machine have to emulate traditional markers of femininity and display them. For example, in the context of the game we have seen questions about length of hair. At the time, long hair was reserved for women and as such could be seen as a marker of femininity. If both the machine and the man pretend to have long hair to pass as a woman, they have understood these markers of femininity and are able to use them to pass as a woman. For a machine to understand the markers of femininity, it would have needed to learn from data that women tend to have long hair and men short hair to then make the prediction that having long hair means that the person is more likely to be a woman. We will delve into questions of how a machine knows who is a woman in Chapter 5 in more detail. For the time being, it suffices to say that reading the Turing Test from a gender and technology perspective opens up novel research questions to investigate in the future.

Research Patterns

In this book, I weave together materials from a range of settings that together form patterns that can inform us about how gender and digitalisation are mutually shaped. I detail my research approach in the appendix. The first research context is books on the future of work that are written for the popular market. I selected books that focused on work and technology. I scanned the business press on book reviews, searched Amazon's recommender system and asked for book recommendations in my professional network. I visited physical bookstores to see what was shelved in sections on the future of work. I also interviewed thought leaders on the future of work. I approached individuals who had a visible presence in discussions about the future of work such as by giving keynotes, being on a panel, giving media interviews or publishing reports. Those individuals worked in international organisations, policy and learned societies. I also spoke to individuals who were working in professional service firms advising clients on the future of work and the field of AI ethics. The findings from the analysis of books and the interviews with thought leaders inform Chapter 2 to illuminate debates on automation and augmentation.

Building on the interviews and the books, I then focused on exploring those areas that were seen as particularly threatened by emerging technologies: the professions. I spoke with individuals working in a range of professions such as audit, tax, legal, consulting, financial technology and architecture. I also spoke to a range of individuals who were experts on so-called new work practices such as holacracy (Robertson, 2015), who could talk about how professional work can be organised in different ways. I was interested to explore which skills are changing in relation to technology and can be trained through technologies such as VR. I was able to conduct a form of auto-ethnography (Hine, 2020; Sparkes, 2003) by using a VR headset (Oculus Quest 2). I undertook training in a range of contexts and settings such as counselling, health and safety, onboarding for people working in grocery stores and leading for inclusion. I analyse this material in Chapter 3 to show which skills are constructed as uniquely human.

Another area that was regularly mentioned particularly in the context of algorithmic bias was using AI in hiring. In this book, I draw on interviews with individuals who worked in areas associated with hiring technologies. These included individuals working in different functions such as those who provide the technology for hiring, those who work in HR functions, and recruiters and hiring consultants. In addition, I tested some of the hiring technologies myself. This included VR recruitment environments, online aptitude and personality tests and asynchronous video interviews. I largely draw on this material in Chapter 4.

The final context from which I draw material relates to how data and gender are intertwined in production processes around AI. My main interest here was on how AI and gender are mutually shaping through processes such as data labelling or data annotation. I spoke to a range of individuals who were involved in the AI production process. Those individuals were, for instance, linguists working in automatic speech recognition, individuals managing data labellers or experts on how AI is created. Some interviewees showed me examples of how data labelling was done and how gender matters in the process, which was helpful to understand these practices. This material is largely covered in Chapter 5.

While all of these contexts are distinct, there was significant overlap between the topics that came to the fore when the material was analysed. As such, the different contexts combine in specific ways to show patterns of gender and digitalisation. These patterns were significantly influenced by being conducted at a specific point in time. This influences which technologies were mentioned as examples. The pandemic itself changed digitalisation substantially and is said to have accelerated digitalisation (Amankwah-Amoah et al., 2021; Schlogl et al., 2021; McKinsey, 2020). Video conferencing moved from a rarely used technology to the standard medium of how work was done during most of the pandemic. Work itself has changed due to the pandemic. Selecting candidates using digital means became a necessity overnight and has, as a consequence, evolved. At the same time, the pandemic meant that the research I was conducting was rather different than I had planned (see the appendix). By weaving different patterns that emerge in these contexts together, this book shows how gender and digitalisation at work operate in different settings and it also shows how these different patterns form a larger picture on gender and digitalisation in the work context.

Structure of the Book

The book is structured into two broad sections. The first section focuses on the discourse of the future of work. In this part of the book, I analyse common tropes used in the books on the future of work and by interviewees such as the man-versus-machine idea and how emotions are constructed as uniquely human. The second part of the book focuses on data and data practices. I analyse how algorithmic bias manifests in relation to hiring and what this means for inclusion. I also show how data practices construct and reconstruct worldviews such as around gender and diversity. Following this introduction, the book is structured into four chapters and a conclusion.

How the future of work is imagined is at the centre of Chapter 2. The chapter analyses how dystopian views emerge in popular books on the future of work, which pitch humans against machines in an epic battle. I discuss this as the man-against-machine trope where machines replace humans. I also show that those who hold at-risk jobs are imagined as men, particularly middle-class men in white-collar professions. The chapter shows how an alternative, possibly more utopian perspective takes hold where humans and machines are not enemies but actually work together. This human–machine collaboration is heralded as a new form of diversity. In this scenario, humans engage in enjoyable and creative tasks whereas machines do the repetitive and mundane work. The books I analysed maintain that socio-emotional skills are out of reach for machines. However, the chapter shows how constructing socio-emotional skills as safe from automation leaves out a wider consideration of how gender, race and class structure current and future inequalities.

In Chapter 3, I continue this line of inquiry by questioning the idea that socio-emotional skills are indeed outside of the realm of machines. This chapter draws on interviews with thought leaders and professionals. I show how drudgework is widely assumed to be automatable because it follows repeatable patterns. I show how the automation of drudgework shifts tasks in professional work and changes structures in professional firms. The chapter shows how socio-emotional skills are constructed as uniquely human because they are seen as out of reach of machines. Looking particularly at examples where machines could be said to engage in socio-emotional skills, I show how machines are trained to recognise human emotions but also how machines train humans in showing appropriate emotions. The chapter argues that socio-emotional skills are following patterns that can be automated and as such do not constitute a competitive advantage of humans over machines. However, if those socio-emotional skills are performed by machines will depend to a large degree on the social desirability of having these tasks performed by machines.

Chapter 4 then engages with the question of how technologies are used in hiring practices. Hiring is a central function of the organisation: it is important to have the right people in place to ensure that the organisation can fulfil its purpose. Yet hiring is also a process fraught with human bias. This is where technology comes in because it promises to make these processes not only more efficient but also more objective. However, technologies have been shown to repeat and amplify exactly these human biases. The chapter traces how a techno-optimist's perspective that technology improves business processes can be reconciled with algorithmic bias. This chapter draws on interviews with experts on the future of work, those who design hiring technologies, as well as my own experiences with those technologies. First, I show that a techno-optimist's stance is the dominant perspective in most of the interviews and that this stance is maintained by constructing algorithmic bias as ultimately fixable. The chapter details how it is suggested that bias emerges from people and which processes and practices are constructed as being able to fix algorithmic bias. I also show that some interviewees displayed what I call techno-hesitation, a wait-and-see stance, which acknowledged that AI-supported hiring will become normalised over time. Overall, the chapter makes the argument that algorithmic bias has to be constructed as ultimately fixable to maintain a techno-optimistic stance.

Chapter 5 traces the question of how a computer knows about the gender of the person. I show that data labelling is central in this process. The chapter centres on two aspects. First, it focuses on who is doing data labelling work. The chapter discusses AI's hidden workforce – those who label data in the AI supply chain. Second, the chapter discusses the constructions of reality that emerge from data labelling. I discuss practices such as how classifications used in data labelling represent specific worldviews. The chapter suggests that what is presented as objective and universal is in fact subjective and partial and as such potentially exclusionary. The chapter suggests that in order to create more inclusionary approaches, it is central to make the underlying processes of constructions that happen in relation to data labelling visible.

Chapter 6 offers a conclusion by weaving different threads that the book uncovered together. I show which future-shaping patterns around digitalisation and gender emerge. The chapter illustrates how seemingly isolated issues form patterns that either hinder or foster inclusion. I speculate how alternative futures might be created. The final chapter also suggests that data is inherently social and thus inevitably biased. However, while this might lead to existing gender patterns being repeated, I suggest that alternative patterns are possible that can be more inclusive.

Conclusion

In this opening chapter of the book, I show how gender, digitalisation and the future of work can be conceived as patterns. Patterns are central for technologies such as machine learning that read existing patterns to predict potential futures. This book focuses on different individual patterns that if brought together show more complex and dynamic patterns of how gender and technology interact in the work context. The chapter started by arguing that how futures of (paid) work are imagined shapes how potential futures might unfold. I then suggested that many new technologies appear magical and mythical to users. I defined key terms for technologies I use in this book and how I employ these terms. In the next section, I explained how I see gender and technology as co-constructed and how seeing gender as performed in and through technologies is a useful lens for this research.

Following this, I outlined how the research was constructed before providing details on how this book is structured. The book weaves together different patterns of gender and technology that emerge in specific settings. By weaving these patterns together, a more nuanced, complex and dynamic pattern of how gender and digitalisation interact in the future of work emerges. The book thus argues that patterns of gender and digitalisation are dynamic and complex but can be used for creating inclusion.

Notes

1 Sex is used in the original.
2 I have discussed differences and similarities of these approaches of how gender is done and performed in detail elsewhere (Kelan, 2009, 2010).

2

IMAGING FUTURES BETWEEN AUTOMATION AND AUGMENTATION

Introduction

Discourses on the future provide templates for how potential futures might unfold. These templates represent patterns based on which thinking of the future is structured. Such discourses of the future regularly play with the contrast between utopian and dystopian visions of the future (Jasanoff, 2015; Schlogl et al., 2021; Howcroft & Taylor, 2023). For discourses on technology at work, these visions manifest in relation to automation and augmentation (Kelan, 2023b; Raisch & Krakowski, 2021). Automation presents a catastrophic view of the future or a dystopia where machines have taken-away jobs that humans used to do, leading to mass unemployment and social unrest. Automation constructs humans and machines as enemies, with both competing for the same work. Augmentation, in contrast, means that humans and machines collaborate to achieve work together by playing to each other's strengths. In this vision of the future, humans and machines collaborate seemingly harmoniously. Humans are said to pivot to skills that

DOI: 10.4324/9781003427100-2

machines are presumed to struggle with: socio-emotional skills. Socio-emotional skills are often seen as something that only humans can do.

In this chapter, we will see how automation and augmentation are not only regularly invoked concepts in the books on the future of work that I analysed, but they also resonate strongly with gender (Kelan, 2023b). Discussions of automation regularly referred the man-versus-machine trope. Furthermore, the jobs that were at risk of automation often belonged to men. The professions were predicted to disappear, yet the role women play in the professions was neglected. Augmentation in contrast was associated with the rise of socio-emotional skills, which were constructed as a core human skill that both women and men can display. Technologies were discussed as gendered, particularly in the context of algorithmic bias. This chapter traces how books on the future of work in relation to automation and augmentation relate to gender. I show how discourses of the future of work replicate some gender patterns but also create new patterns. This chapter discusses the contours of some of the patterns that will be discussed in greater detail throughout the book.

Visions of the Future of Work

Prior to the Covid-19 pandemic, one of the most pressing questions regularly asked in the media was 'will a robot take your job?'. The idea of robots stealing jobs is an established trope in discussions about technology. Such discussions are often followed by a mention of Luddites destroying textile machinery. These images pitch humans against machines. As machines are deployed, humans lose their jobs. Although research has shown that automation replaces and creates new work (Autor, 2015; Autor et al., 2023), the idea that humans are replaced by the latest technologies associated with digitalisation permeates popular imaginaries such as the multitude of reports on the future of work (OECD, 2016; Frey & Osborne, 2017; Manyika, Chui, et al., 2017; Manyika, Lund, et al., 2017). These worrying scenarios about the future of work seem to suggest that mass unemployment will destabilise economies and societies unless urgent policy interventions are taken. The Covid-19 pandemic has, at least temporarily, called into question such scenarios. Instead, ideas such as the 'great resignation' and the 'great attrition' suggest that people no longer want to work like before the pandemic (De Smet et al., 2021; Serenko, 2022). However, these ideas re-emerged when ChatGPT started being used widely; it was speculated that this technology might mean the end of professional work (Mollick, 2022; Roose, 2022). This shows the enduring appeal of discussing automation as a force that takes away jobs from humans. In fact, many writers on the future of work recognise that prior dystopian predictions of jobless futures have not come to pass but go on to insist that 'this time it is different'. This trope of 'this time it is different' has been identified in earlier research to create a sense of urgency that change is afoot and that we need to react now to avoid the catastrophic visions of the future coming to pass (Wajcman, 2017; Howcroft & Rubery, 2019).

The future of work has also inspired countless books on that topic that fall mainly into category of business and management books. Many of those books centre specifically on technology to analyse how technology might shape the future of work. When analysing management books on the future of work in relation to technology, Raisch and Krakowski (2021) found that an automation perspective is indeed dominating such books. However, they also showed that an alternative perspective is also gaining prominence: augmentation (Raisch & Krakowski, 2021). Augmentation entails that humans and machines collaborate to get work done, which is said to lead to superior business performance (Raisch & Krakowski, 2021). While there is a strong tendency to see automation and augmentation as an either/or choice, Raisch and Krakowski (2021) stress that automation and augmentation coexist across place and time.

The concepts of automation and augmentation resonated strongly in the corpus of literature that I analysed. Since I wanted to find out how gender is discussed in the literature on the future of work, I started by searching the business press, such as The Economist, The New York Times, The Wall Street Journal and the Financial Times, for book reviews or book recommendations. I also used Amazon's recommendation system to source similar books and, prior to the pandemic, also visited physical bookstores to see which other books were shelved in similar sections. I also looked for books that were written by well-known writers on the future of work. Finally, I asked my network for book recommendations.

The books I selected fulfil all of the following criteria: the books should be addressed to the general public, focus on general work and its intersections with technology (widely defined as digitalisation, machine learning, AI, automation and robotics) and should be written in English.

I included books published from 2017 to 2020, which capture the market just prior to the pandemic. Even though some books had been published during the early phase of the pandemic, in most cases, they only included cursory references to Covid-19. A notable first finding is that none of these books were written by women. The books written by women did not focus on work and were more general, or they were more specific in focusing, for instance, on the gig economy. I analysed the following ten books:

- Richard Baldwin (2019) *The Globotics Upheaval: Globalization, Robotics and the Future of Work.*
- Aaron Benanav (2020) *Automation and the Future of Work.*
- David de Cremer (2020) *Leadership by Algorithm: Who Leads and Who Follows in the AI Era?*
- Paul Daugherty and H. James Wilson (2018) *Human + Machine: Reimagining Work in the Age of AI.*
- Carl Benedikt Frey (2019), *The Technology Trap: Capital, Labor, and Power in the Age of Automation.*
- Andrew McAfee and Erik Brynjolfsson (2017) *Machine, Platform, Crowd: Harnessing Our Digital Future.*
- Jamie Merisotis (2020) *Human Work In the Age of Smart Machines.*
- Klaus Schwab (2018) *Shaping the Future of the Fourth Industrial Revolution.*
- Daniel Susskind (2020) *A World Without Work: Technology, Automation and How We Should Respond.*
- Darrell M. West (2018) *The Future of Work: Robots, AI, and Automation.*

For ease of reading, in this chapter, I refer to the book authors by surname.

In the following, I discuss how the discourses of the future of work create patterns of how the future of work is imagined, and many of those patterns are meaningful to understand how gender is constructed.

This Time It Is Different

The common tenor in the book I analysed was that the future of work will bring significant changes, and there is a strong sentiment across the books that 'this time it is different'. This has previously been identified as a common discursive formation in discussions of the future of work

(Wajcman, 2017; Howcroft & Rubery, 2019). The discursive formation presented in the books is formed partly by citing 'smart experts', who warn about the speed of job displacements, the perils of new technology and the end of humanity and civilisation. Three individuals are commonly used for this purpose: Bill Gates (Baldwin, Benanav and de Cremer), Elon Musk (Baldwin, Benanav and West) and Stephen Hawking (Baldwin, de Cremer and Frey). McAfee and Brynjolfsson's earlier book, *The Second Machine Age* (McAfee & Brynjolfsson, 2014), is regularly referenced, for example, by Benanav, Frey, Schwab and West, and of course, by McAfee and Brynjolfsson themselves. Merisotis mentions Klaus Schwab and Richard Baldwin. This indicates that each of the authors draws on similar individuals to make the case why urgent action has to be taken to avoid that catastrophic futures of work come to pass.

The expected changes in the future of work are also put in the context of different industrial revolutions. The most well-known example is how Schwab talks about the Fourth Industrial Revolution. For Schwab, the First Industrial Revolution refers to the mechanisation of the textile industry in Britain. The Second Industrial Revolution is associated with the telephone, electricity and the automobile. The Third Industrial Revolution centres on digital computing. The Fourth Industrial Revolution entails a range of new technologies, which include AI, distributed ledgers (blockchain), advanced materials, and virtual and augmented realities. Schwab predicts that exponential growth in these new technologies will lead to rapid change. This rapid change means, for instance, that automation progresses, which in turn accelerates job losses. Similarly, McAfee and Brynjolfsson talk about industrial revolutions when talking about the 'second machine age'. The first machine age was the Industrial Revolution, when machines started to support and replace human labour. The second machine age started in the mid-1990s with digitalisation. It is characterised by machines not simply following rules but solving problems on their own. Thus, machines now perform cognitive tasks previously reserved for humans.

Discussions of expected changes in the future of work are commonly framed from the perspective of historical technical transformations, such as the shift from horses to cars (Frey, Susskind and Baldwin) and electrification (Frey, McAfee and Brynjolfsson). It is also common to reference specific jobs such as work in banks. It is, for instance, stressed that automatic teller machines (ATMs) changed bank tellers' work rather than making them redundant (Susskind). Yet, it is also acknowledged that online banking may reduce demand for bank tellers (Frey). Other jobs mentioned include elevator operators (Susskind and Frey), whose jobs were superseded by automation. However, the replacement of elevator operators caused strong concern for passengers because humans were no longer responsible for people's safety (Susskind and Frey).

Some of the technologies are also discussed in relation to gender. For example, the typewriter is used as an illustration for office mechanisation and women's work (Frey). Schwab and Frey discuss household mechanisation and its impact on women, who, as they state, were previously responsible for such tasks. A common narrative is that mechanisation of the household freed women to join the labour market. However, both Frey and Schwab observe that the time that women spent on household tasks did not decrease but that household mechanisation tended to mean that domestic servants were replaced by technology.

It is also widely acknowledged that such transformations were associated with a backlash against technology. For instance, Baldwin suggests that transformations produce upheavals, leading to a backlash before a resolution is achieved. Susskind mentioned the Luddites in this context. Others point out that if alternative job options are available, technology is met with less resistance (Frey). Backlashes are also commonly discussed in relation to neoliberalism and austerity (Benavav), and the election of Donald Trump as president of the United States (West). The argument seems to be that few transformations occur without resistance, but that such resistance disappears over time as the new *status quo* is achieved.

The 'this time it is different' trope is used largely to make a case that urgent action must be taken to shape these changes. For instance, Frey seeks to be guided by history, suggesting that a core message of his book is that we have been in similar situations before and thus know how to react. Susskind acknowledges that jobs being replaced by technology is a common fear, which, however, has thus far failed to come to pass. In spite of this disclaimer, Susskind continues with the caveat that even though 'this time is different' did not prove right before, it might still come true now. Schwab's book features expert commentaries, such as from Richard Soley, chairman and chief executive officer (CEO) of Object Management Group, who observes that technology has been evolutionary rather than revolutionary in the past, but he warns that this time it is different.

To support their calls for action, the authors commonly refer to the speed and scale of the transformations. In a section of his book, entitled 'Why this time is different', Baldwin explains that his main areas of concern of globalisation and robotics, which he summarises as globotics, are by no means new areas of concern. However, what is different now and what Baldwin uses to create as his reason why this time it is different is that these changes come fast. Additionally, he states that people perceive them as unfair because the ability to earn an income is taken away from them. McAfee and Brynjolfsson suggest in a similar vein that while these technology-driven changes are not new as such, prior changes took longer to take place and did not affect a global economy. Schwab suggests that the Fourth Industrial Revolution accelerates faster because it can build on the digital infrastructure of the Third Industrial Revolution. Thus, 'this time it is different' is used to describe both the speed and scope of transformation.

There is a consensus that the transformations will have a strong impact on jobs that will disappear due to automation. Four studies are commonly cited to support this claim. First, the Oxford Martin Programme's study on 'The Future of Employment' (Frey & Osborne, 2017), which suggests that 47% of US employment is at risk of automation. Second, a policy brief by the Organisation for Economic Co-operation and Development (OECD, 2016), entitled 'Automation and Independent Work in a Digital Economy', which suggests that a fairly small percentage of jobs is at risk of being automated (9%), although a further quarter of jobs will have half of their tasks changed due to automation. Finally, two reports by the McKinsey Global Institute, entitled 'A Future that Works' (Manyika, Chui, et al., 2017) and 'Jobs Lost, Jobs Gained' (Manyika, Lund, et al., 2017), find that almost half of the activities that currently constitute paid work might be done by machines, and that between 3% and 14% of the global workforce will need to switch occupational categories due to automation.

While the evaluation of the different methodologies and predictions of these four studies is beyond the scope of this chapter, it is interesting to note that the books I analysed regularly drew on these studies. These studies were mobilised in the books to support the claim that jobs will be lost due to these transformations. The studies cited in the books are thus an important rhetorical device to support the claims that the authors of the books make. Baldwin believes that automation will change jobs but not occupations, and Frey and Merisotis suggest that tasks rather than occupations will be automated. Similarly, Schwab states that AI will change tasks rather than making people redundant. Based on these scenarios, the arguments made in the books focus on suggestions that the future will see less paid work (Susskind) or too many people for too few jobs (Benanav). Job losses and associated changes to the economy thus take centre stage. These messages are supported by the idea that while technology has led to economic change before, this time it is different.

It is notable that this discourse of 'this time it is different' makes such a strong appearance in the books, which aligns with earlier research (Wajcman, 2017; Howcroft & Rubery, 2019). The 'this time it is different' trope creates a sense of urgency that action has to be taken to avoid that the catastrophic versions of the future come to pass. In order to avoid mass unemployment, the books represent a call to business people and policymakers to take action now to build futures that avoid these catastrophic visions of the future. They provide a burning platform that can be a driver for change. Using such discourses is additionally a way to sell such popular books. Moreover, the interplay between dystopia and utopia is strategically employed in these books to paint two versions of the future, where one is undesirable and the other one is desirable. However, in order to get to the desirable future, the right action has to be taken now to avoid the undesirable alternative.

Man-versus-Machine

In order to express anxieties around automation, the books regularly use the trope of man-versus-machine. The man-versus-machine trope is popular and deployed in six of the books in slightly different variations. The trope constructs men and machine as rivals. The trope is well established in popular culture, such as 2001: A Space Odyssey and The Terminator. Such movies are contributing to the imagination that the future entails an epic (and gendered) battle between man and machine. In relation to the work context, that means that a machine competes with man to eventually replace him. The idea that an epic battle between human and machine takes place is expressed through the idea of competitive games that are regularly used. Alpha Go, a computer that plays the board game Go, is for instance referenced by Baldwin, Benanav, de Cremer, Frey, McAfee and Brynjolfsson, and Schwab, and often discussed in the context of the human being beaten by the machine that has become intelligent enough to do so.

The man-versus-machine trope also finds its expression in automation anxiety, which de Cremer, Schwab and Susskind use to refer to the fear that a robot might take your job. The idea that there is less work left for humans is also central in Merisotis' book. De Cremer concludes that the thinking of man-versus-machine, together with scientific evidence on automation anxiety, centres most discussions on AI's potential to replace people's jobs. In a similar vein, Susskind suggests that machines continually improve their performance, which limits activities where humans have the edge. For Susskind, this challenges the idea that humans are superior and could not be replaced. Instead, he suggests that an 'inferiority assumption' might be more accurate in that machines rather than humans become the norm for performing tasks.

A variation of automation anxiety that Daugherty and Wilson and de Cremer reference is algorithm aversion. Daugherty and Wilson describe algorithm aversion as the phenomenon that people trust humans more than machines, whereas de Cremer notes that it means that people avoid taking advice from algorithms. De Cremer explains the suspicion towards algorithms with the metaphor of the black box. Given the fact that algorithms function like black boxes, people are sceptical about algorithms making autonomous decisions. In fact, the black box idea is another common metaphor used that appears in five books (Baldwin, Daugherty and Wilson, Schwab, West, and of course, de Cremer, as discussed previously). It commonly describes that the recommendations that algorithms make are opaque, even to those who design those systems. The lack of explainability is a problem that Daugherty and Wilson, and Baldwin mention. West, in contrast, refers to how the European Union's General Data Protection Regulation is addressing the black box by giving individuals insight into how the black box operates. The black box metaphor, together with a discussion of algorithm aversion, is mobilised to explain why automation anxiety is a concern.

However, while the man-versus-machine trope is regularly found in the books I analysed to express automation anxiety, I also found that augmentation as humans and machines collaborating was discussed in the books.

Daugherty and Wilson are possibly the most explicit in that they transform the man-versus-machine trope into human + machine to argue for the value of augmentation. It is also notable that in the book title, Daugherty and Wilson use human + machine, which challenges the rather exclusionary notion of the man-versus-machine trope. In some instances, they talk about man + machine as a direct contrast to man versus machine. Daugherty and Wilson explain that it is common to see humans and machines as rivals where machines steal humans' jobs. However, in their book, they stress that machines and humans collaborate, which represents augmentation rather than automation and replacement. Similarly, de Cremer presumes that humans and machines will collaborate, and he calls this the new diversity. De Cremer writes an entire section about this new diversity. Notably, diversity is not referring to diversity among humans, but this new diversity that de Cremer describes lies between humans and machines. Like with human–human diversity, de Cremer cautions that human–machine diversity will appear alien to many humans. This is due to the fact that we have been conditioned to think about humans and machines as antagonists rather than as symbiotic. As such, this new form of diversity is in fact resonating with augmentation.

Given the popularity of the man-versus-machine trope in popular culture, it is not surprising that the trope was regularly used in the books I analysed. The man-versus-machine trope was invoked directly but also indirectly; for instance, when the black box of AI and algorithmic aversion was discussed. However, it is notable that augmentation was presented as an alternative to automation, where machines replace humans. In fact, this augmentation was talked about as new diversity, where diversity refers to humans and machines collaborating. Yet, even these collaborations between humans and machines were marred by the potential negative impact of humans seeing machines as enemy. The obvious criticism of the man-versus-machine trope is that it could be read as gender exclusionary. While clearly, some authors make attempts to be more gender inclusive by using human + machine, the man-versus-machine trope is largely used to articulate automation anxiety and to show how augmentation might be hampered by humans feeling hostile to technology. I will now turn to understanding in a more granular way who is expected to lose out in this epic battle between humans and machines.

Men's Jobs

In the previous section, we have seen how the man-versus-machine trope is commonly used to express automation anxieties. I will now show that it is men who are constructed as at risk of seeing their jobs disappear. The risk that men might lose their jobs is leading to a heightened concern for the future of work. For example, Frey states that it is men who are more likely to be replaced by robots than women. There is also concern that men in their prime will face redundancy but lack the flexibility in their identities to move to alternative jobs, as Susskind says. This affects men in white- and blue-collar jobs and thus spans different class backgrounds. As such, the argument that men who lose their jobs are unable to find new work, which affects their sense of self, has to be read in the context of men's traditional role in society. Men's traditional role in Western societies entails being a breadwinner. This is, for instance, addressed by Benanav. Benanav suggests that the concept of the male breadwinner as the head of the household, and women as the main caregivers earning supplemental incomes, is deeply enshrined in the sociocultural fabric of many economies. He cites mini-jobs in Germany, which he suggests are effectively designed to be done by stay-at-home wives, whose incomes supplement those of the main male breadwinners. This traditional arrangement is rewarded by the state through tax incentives.

The gender-segregated nature of the workforce, with men and women being clustered in different jobs, or references to how women and men might be positioned in these new futures of work, is at best marginal in the books. However, Frey and Susskind discuss pink-collar work. Pink-collar work has traditionally been done by women and is therefore associated with the colour pink. Susskind alludes to the fact that the naming of pink-collar work is unfortunate. He goes on to explain that men who miss out on blue-collar work are often unwilling to take on pink-collar work. He describes this as problematic because many pink-collar jobs are at the moment out of reach of machines. Frey in turn discusses how pink-collar work became more important with the introduction of the typewriter. He here links job growth to mechanisation. At the same time, he acknowledges that the growth of the pink-collar workforce came to an end in the 2000s as computers became ubiquitous. However, he does not see these trends as affecting women negatively because he states that women made inroads into well-paid jobs, so much so that, as he states, younger women in the United States now out-earn their male counterparts. Overall, these constructions leave the reader with the impression that women are doing well, in spite of automation threats. Yet, there is a concern for men who lose their jobs but are not flexible enough in their identities to take on other types of work that are seeing growth because such work is associated with women.

In this section, we have seen that men's jobs, both in blue- and white-collar jobs, are constructed as particularly at threat of automation. Women's jobs in contrast are not seen as under threat of automation. Pink-collar work, for instance, is constructed as future-proof and it is also stated that women in generally do well professionally. This leaves the reader with the impression that we need to focus on the demise of men's jobs. While blue-collar jobs are affected by automation and have been affected by it for a long time, a new threat is identified in the books: the threat to white-collar jobs.

Disappearing Professions

Although both blue- and white-collar jobs are constructed as at risk, it is particularly white-collar work that many of the authors of the future of work books focus on. White-collar work is largely seen as desirable work in the books. Baldwin states, historically, blue-collar jobs were affected by automation, which means that white-collar and professional jobs were sheltered from robots and globalisation until now. He focuses specifically on white-collar robots that are replacing middle-class jobs. Although white-collar robots are not yet as good as white-collar humans, robots are simply more cost effective: Baldwin states that a white-collar robot costs a fifth of a worker in the developed world and a third of a worker in less developed areas. It should be noted that white-collar robots will not take over entire occupations. However, they might well take over specific tasks, which over time can reduce the need for human white-collar workers overall.

White-collar and professional jobs are also those that require an upfront investment into education that is then paying off with higher lifetime earnings. Benanav describes this as the idea that a good education will lead to and ensure a good middle-class job. However, the idea that a good education will lead to a good middle-class job is now changing, according to the books I analysed. Similarly, Susskind talks about the signalling entailed in having a good college degree. Whereas in the past, a good college degree would be important to find a job and climb the occupational ladder, the good college degree has lost its significance. Frey provides a rationale why white-collar work is well paid: he argues that in the Second Industrial Revolution, the opportunity costs for education decreased because higher-level skills were in demand; as a result, white-collar workers were paid well for their education. A dramatic change is now that a good education no longer guarantees that individuals can achieve and sustain a middle-class lifestyle. If middle-class workers are being replaced by technology, this is expected to have wide-ranging effects. Frey, for instance, presumes that the replacement of middle-class workers by machines will decrease demand for local services. Earlier redundancies are constructed as having had limited effects, as it was possible to find other professional jobs elsewhere. A central concern of future-of-work writers is thus that securing a prosperous future by investing in educational credentials no longer applies.

The link between education and career is nowhere more visible than in the professions. Baldwin details that professional jobs were sheltered from globalisation and robots because they required face-to-face contact, which no longer is the case. Benanav cites Robert Reich's contention that technology is replacing professional jobs, and Schwab suggests that automation is now replacing professional workers such as accountants and lawyers rather than factory workers. The books mention professional work in finance (Baldwin, de Cremer and Schwab) and accounting (Frey, Schwab and Merisotis). However, the profession attracting the most attention is legal work, which is discussed in seven books. Baldwin provides various examples of how legal work is being automated using software, such as Lex Machina and Ravel Law, which helps to sort through information and even suggests legal strategies. This means that many tasks that junior lawyers would have traditionally done are now automated. Baldwin summarises that whereas a law degree was a secure way to ensure middle-class prosperity, white-collar robots are now competing with junior lawyers. According to de Cremer, in the legal world, automated advisors are used to contest parking tickets, and Susskind observes that automated document review systems can scan material more swiftly and often more accurately. Susskind mentions how a law firm uses software to reduce the time human lawyers have to spend on tasks. West mentions an AI-driven bankruptcy legal assistant. Most of the books suggest that legal work is at high risk of automation, and only Frey voices a dissenting view. Although Frey acknowledges that legal libraries are available online, he cites a study calculating that only 13% of legal tasks can actually be automated, supporting his own prediction that legal work is at low risk of being automated.

The common tenor in the books is that professional jobs where education is rewarded are disappearing. These professional jobs are presumed to be held by men. This is not to say that these books are unaware that women take professional jobs. In fact, the books strongly signal gender awareness. For instance, authors are regularly citing stories of an engineer, a professor, a software developer or a surgeon who turn out to use the pronoun 'she'. By using the pronoun 'she', the authors break the implicit assumption that these professional jobs are held by men only. However, what is missing from the discussions is an acknowledgement that women have made in-roads into professional work. Of course, these professions, as much research has shown, are far from gender inclusive (Ely, 1995; Walsh, 2012; Lupu, 2012; Kokot-Blamey, 2021, 2023). However, most books fail to discuss the fact that the professions have become more diverse over the years and women, in particular, are increasingly present in the professions. By not discussing how the gender presentation has changed the professions in greater detail, readers will be left with the impression that these jobs are held by men. This is particularly the case because men in general are singled out as particularly affected by the automation, as we have seen in the previous section.

A second aspect that is rarely discussed is how the professions are changing. While some authors predict the death of the professions, at least Frey seemed more sceptical in regard to what the future of the legal profession holds. However, in reality, the professions might be transformed with some aspects being done with the help of technology, while other tasks might gain more prominence. As such, the content of professional work might change, requiring substantial changes in regard to how professional work is organised and how training is structured in those firms. While most of these questions are beyond the scope of the books analysed, I will revisit some of those questions in Chapter 3.

Socio-Emotional Skills as Human Advantage

It is evident that the dystopian images used in the future of work books I analysed relate to automation and particularly the automation of professional jobs. Yet, some of the books also sketch the contours of a more utopian future of work. This entails that humans and machine collaborate and enhance each other's skills. In other words, the books talk about augmentation (Kelan, 2023b; Raisch & Krakowski, 2021). Another area that the books address are those jobs that are out of reach of machines. These jobs are constructed as future-proof. Both the jobs that are augmented by technologies and those that are safe from automation share in common that they rely on a specific set of human skills. I call these skills socio-emotional skills and will discuss in this section how these socio-emotional skills are constructed as the key competitive advantage that humans have over machines.

By and large, the skills that are said to be future-proof are those that are seen as difficult for machines to accomplish. These include leadership (de Cremer, McAfee and Brynjolfsson), teamwork (McAfee and Brynjolfsson), creativity (De Cremer, Merisotis and Schwab), coaching (McAfee and Brynjolfsson) and, in general, anything that requires socio-emotional skills. I use socio-emotional skills because the authors of the book have different names for such skills. For example, Merisotis cites Anne-Marie Slaughter saying that the economic formation has moved from hiring hands over hiring heads to hiring hearts, where hearts are used to present socio-emotional skills. McAfee and Brynjolfsson use the example that when receiving a medical diagnosis, people prefer to receive those from compassionate people rather than machines. This means that compassion is constructed as a desirable skill in humans. Susskind uses the term 'social intelligence' and states that technologies cannot deal with tasks requiring social intelligence well, such as providing empathy or face-to-face interaction. De Cremer argues that algorithms lack what he calls social skills. Baldwin, Merisotis, McAfee and Brynjolfsson, and Schwab talk about social and interpersonal skills, Baldwin and Susskind about social intelligence, De Cremer about emotional intelligence, and De Cremer, Merisotis, McAfee and Baldwin also use empathy. Given the fact that authors use a range of terms to describe such skills, I use socio-emotional skills as an umbrella term for these skills. It is socio-emotional skills that are constructed as uniquely human and as hard to replace by machines.

The books construct jobs that entail socio-emotional skills as safe from automation. These include medicine (Frey), teaching (Baldwin and Susskind) and social work (Susskind). Another area of growth are personal services, which entails beach body coaches, yoga instructors and Zumba instructors, which are mentioned in various combinations by Susskind, West, McAfee and Brynjolfsson, and Frey. Common to these areas of work is motivating people through socio-emotional support, and the assumption is that machines could not provide this socio-emotional support. It is interesting that these particular areas of work are used to illustrate the importance of socio-emotional skills, while changes in the professions towards more socio-emotional skills were rarely discussed.

The rise of socio-emotional skills is of course not new. As a matter of fact, I explored this in earlier research, where I analysed the books on the future of work that existed at the time (Kelan, 2008b). In those books, it was notable that socio-emotional skills were constructed as feminine and presumed to reside in women. Yet, this was not the case in the current batch of books that I analysed for this research. The closest of such association was in relation to paid care work. Susskind and West, for instance, mention that women often work in caring professions, and Susskind even points out that caring work is often undervalued. One could now presume that care work is safe from automation, which is indeed alluded to. However, West casts some doubt on whether such jobs are indeed future-proof. West references that technology is changing care giving. This might mean that socio-emotional skills might eventually also cease to be central for care-giving roles, but this was an opinion that was not predominant. Overall, the image that emerges in the books is that socio-emotional skills are uniquely human. As a consequence, jobs that require socio-emotional skills are constructed as safe from automation. Whereas earlier research has shown how socio-emotional skills are often presumed but not rewarded in women, in these books, socio-emotional skills are presented as gender neutral and as if everyone could engage in them. I will return to the question of if socio-emotional skills are indeed uniquely human in Chapter 3.

Creating the Human–Machine Interface

After discussing the presumed importance of socio-emotional skills, I would now like to discuss how machines and humans collaborate or augment one another. I will focus particularly on technical professions here because they are regularly mentioned in the books. The authors call this the human–machine interface (Baldwin, Naughty and De Cremer), which includes machine learning engineers, data scientists and big data architects (Frey). Commonly, these areas of work appear far removed from socio-emotional skills. However, as we will see, the way these areas of work are described indicates that they rely on a form of socio-emotional skills. Daugherty and Wilson, in particular, describe how machine learning programmers are becoming more like teachers who train the algorithms. This is different to how programming was traditionally perceived – as writing code that a machine executes. Now, a programmer seems akin to a teacher, who teaches not children but machines.

Most of the books are concerned with high-end AI work. The books discuss the skills shortage in jobs related to AI, which is said to limit the development in the field (Baldwin). This means that too few humans are able to do these highly skilled jobs that are required to make AI function. However, rather than training more individuals, the solution he suggests recurs to technology. Baldwin suggests that Google's automated machine learning, where machines train other machines, might be a solution for this skills shortage.

However, Daugherty and Wilson also discuss how new technologies require other experts that have specific skill sets that one might not traditionally associate with technology work. Such experts know about human conversation, humour and empathy. Those experts can teach the technology to emulate socio-emotional skills. Daugherty and Wilson provide a range of examples of such roles: a poet, novelist and playwright at Microsoft's Cortana and a vehicle design anthropologist at Nissan. This socio-emotional work for machines appears to be needed in order to design technology with which humans enjoy engaging and that is fit for purpose. To achieve this, technology must emulate humans, and according to Daugherty and Wilson, humans are best placed to enable this. This means that many emerging jobs will provide a sort of affective labour for machines.

There is comparatively little discussion about the demographic background of those who design AI in the books. Schwab mentions that women hold less than 25% of IT jobs. This is problematic for him because it means that many ideas are not considered, which in turn is constructed as a hindrance for the development of what he calls the Fourth Industrial Revolution. However, apart from that, the lack of diversity in regard to gender and other dimensions of difference is rarely discussed. This is notable because if there is a skills shortage, it is commonly claimed that women should be mobilised to take these roles, particularly if they involve a socio-emotional skills component. However, such suggestions are not commonly made in the books.

Another area that seems less well discussed in the books is the work in AI supply chains. In contrast to the much in-demand designers of AI, jobs that involve preparing data for machine learning through, for instance, data labelling or data annotation, are rarely discussed. The notable exception is the book by Daugherty and Wilson, which references the work that can easily be outsourced or crowd-sourced, such as training AI. We will return to how such types of work intersect with gender in Chapter 5.

Although the skills shortage in relation to AI work is regularly invoked in the books, there are also signs that the traditional jobs associated with creating emerging technologies are changing. It is suggested that parts of programming jobs can be automated by machines programming them-selves — or rather using tools that generate code. As mentioned before, programmers are presumed to become like teachers or trainers. Additionally, experts on socio-emotional skills will be required to teach machines how to communicate with humans. However, we have also seen that the gender composition of these jobs is often neglected. Similarly, less high-end work such as that required to prepare data for machine learning is less regularly the focus of attention.

Gendered by Design

Gender and technology are not at the core of any of the books, but some of the books do provide interesting illustrations of how gender is entered into the debate. Schwab, in particular, discusses what is akin to technology being gendered by design. Schwab suggests that how machines are pro-grammed and how they interact is impacted by sexism and racism. In his view, robots, particularly humanoid robots, are no longer bound by race and gender when they are designed. Yet, customer service robots often dis-play female characteristics and industrial robots feature male characteristics. In Schwab's view, rather than challenging old stereotypes, the same stereo-types are repeated. He argues that the well-being of all individuals would be increased if more conscious choices are made during the development of technologies, which would then avoid repeating the same stereotypes.

Baldwin offers two examples of gender that are relevant to technology. Baldwin observes that people have a tendency to give nicknames
to robots, unlike other devices that they might use, such as smartphones
or Microsoft Excel. He explains this by referring to social psychologists
who talk about 'attribution'; this for him means that as soon as objects
move, people tend to attribute meaning to those objects. Here, movement is
presented as leading to anthropomorphising by giving the software a nick-
name. Baldwin describes the example of Poppy, a white-collar robot that is
employed at Lloyd's of London. Poppy's human co-worker gave the robot
its name. He also discusses the example of a remote worker who has a robot
to take her place in the company. The remote worker, Emily Dreyfus, called
the robot EmBot. Baldwin describes an incident of 'inappropriate robot
touching' (Baldwin, 2019, p. 136), which resonates strongly with traditional forms of sexual harassment. When the EmBot was at work, someone
in the office picked up the robot and shook it, which made the operator of
the robot feel powerless and violated. This meant that the company, Wired,
introduced a rule that when the EmBot is activated, it can only be touched
after prior permission from the operator. However, robot touching is only
inappropriate when Dreyfus is 'in the machine', and without Dreyfus in the
machine, it is apparently okay to touch the robot inappropriately.

There is another gendered example in Baldwin's book: Tiffany, a virtual assistant in a Mercedes dealership in Texas, who customers apparently
loved so much that they brought roses for the virtual assistant or tried
to ask 'her' on a date. While these remarks were probably made in jest, it
goes to show that gendered female robots are sexualised just like human
women. Interestingly, while sex robots are often discussed in relation to
technology and gender (Devlin & Belton, 2020), only West mentions sex
robots.

There were also some subtle and not spelled out gender connotations
attached to training AI. Daugherty and Wilson mention research at
DeepMind, where an AI played one game that involved hunting and the
other involved gathering. After playing the hunting game, the AI exhibited
highly aggressive behaviour. After playing the gathering game, the AI
displayed cooperation. While gender is not explicitly mentioned here, the
connotations of aggression versus cooperation and hunting versus gathering
has a potentially gendered subtext in popular perception: aggressiveness is
often associated with masculinity, whereas cooperation is associated with

femininity. This specific example then alludes to the idea that an AI might learn about gender in more indirect ways. One could speculate that if an AI is trained through such games, the AI will also learn about gender in society and replicate a specific and in many ways stereotypical way in which behaviours are considered as gendered.

Overall, examples of gender and technology were few and far between in the books. The few examples that exist show that exploring some of dynamics of gendered by design in greater detail is important to understand gender patterns in the future of work. The section has also shown how stereotypes enter the design of machines in more or less direct ways. This suggests that the resulting technologies were deeply intertwined with how gender is seen in society, which are thereby perpetuated into the future.

Algorithmic Bias

While generally, gender was not something that the book discussed in greater detail, there was one topic that came up regularly: algorithmic bias. Six of the books mention algorithmic bias (Daugherty and Wilson, De Cremer, McAfee and Brynjolfsson, Schwab, Susskind and West). Algorithmic bias can thus be understood as one central way in which issues of inequalities are discussed in the literature I analysed.

When discussing how algorithmic bias develops, most of the authors tend to agree that the reason lies in the data used for machine learning. Schwab suggests data sets reflect human bias, which in turn leads to algorithmic bias. Schwab says that there are many cases of algorithms creating inaccurate responses, which he attributes to misspecification and unrepresentative training data. Similarly, West points to historical data bias by stating that historical data sets mirror traditional values, which, however, might or might not be aligned with what is desired in the current system. West thus explains how historical bias also reflects values, and as those values change, the machine learning might be out of date. This is echoed by Daugherty and Wilson, who paraphrase the computer adage 'garbage in, garbage out' (Weyerer & Langer, 2019) by stating that the quality of an AI system is due to the data it is trained on. As AI systems search for patterns, biases in the data are reflected in the outputs or, as they say, 'biases in, biases out' (Daugherty & Wilson, 2018, p. 121).

While the authors agree how algorithmic bias emerges, they are divided about how to mitigate algorithmic bias. De Cremer, for example, suggests that humans can self-correct if they are biased. This is due to the fact that humans have empathy. However, according to De Cremer, algorithms lack empathy and can thus not self-correct. Furthermore, de Cremer insists that humans are good at spotting bias. Algorithms, in contrast, de Cremer suggests, learn from observable trends. However, McAfee and Brynjolfsson suggest that machines can correct for bias. They describe how testing and improving machine-based systems is an opportunity to correct mistakes. Once corrected, the machine would not make the same mistake, in this case bias, again. McAfee and Brynjolfsson believe that it is more difficult for humans to overcome biases. McAfee and Brynjolfsson recognise the fact that AI might replicate and amplify biases but they also suggest that if those mistakes are corrected, such biases would not be repeated again.

The books provide a range of examples of how algorithmic bias can affect society in general and organisations more specifically. Susskind references a well-known example of racism in regard to an image labelling technology: Black people were labelled as gorillas. McAfee and Brynjolfsson mention that if you conduct an image search for 'scientist' or 'grandmother', most of the images show white people. The example of searching for 'loving grandmother' and being offered images of white women is also mentioned by Daugherty and Wilson. As such, a common example for algorithmic bias relates to images being offered by search engines.

West also cites failure rates in facial recognition as one area where gender and race are interviewed. Specifically, West references Joy Buolamwini's work, which has shown how women with darker skin tones are often mis-classified. Buolamwini and Gebru (2018) have shown that darker-skinned women are misclassified with significantly higher error than white-skinned men. This is attributed to the fact that the database that automated facial recognition technologies were trained on consisted largely of men with lighter skin tones.

Daugherty and Wilson (2018) use the example of credit approval based on geographic locations, which traditionally meant that biases in regard to gender, race or postal code would be taken into account, but by having more complete data, such biases can be avoided. Another example that is mentioned relates to Airbnb. McAfee and Brynjolfsson cite Airbnb CEO and co-founder Joe Gebbia saying that hosts are more likely to select white guests than guests belonging to a minority background, but that reversed if the minority guests have more than ten reviews and a good overall rating.

This, for Joe Gebbia, as referenced in McAfee and Brynjolfsson, means that reputation is more important than similarity.

One of the most widely used examples in the books is the use of AI in hiring. McAfee and Brynjolfsson mention this in regard to the fact that Google's automated, ad-serving algorithm started associating certain ads with Black-sounding names, which might impact which job adverts people see. Similarly, West refers to research that shows that Google advertises executive positions to men rather than women, making it difficult for women to see and apply for such positions. Merisotis discusses how one organisation, Catalyte, is using data to select candidates that were traditionally overlooked as potential programmers, for instance, due to race. While Merisotis is not discussing Catalyte in the context of algorithmic bias as such, he shows how Catalyte is using data and AI to reduce existing inequalities. De Cremer mentions how Amazon tried to apply algorithms in hiring and the algorithm suggested white men due to the fact that learning from past job-performance data, the algorithm learned that white men were the best performers. However, in de Cremer's view, that is problematic because in the past, the majority of workers were white men but that norms in regard to diversity have changed. De Cremer points out how this means that organisations might simply replicate existing populations; human bias is solidified in who was hired in the past.

The analysis of the books has shown that algorithmic bias is one of the most frequently discussed issues in relation to gender. We have seen that data is seen as responsible for producing this bias, but that once corrected, such biases could be eradicated permanently. We will revisit these ideas around algorithmic bias as they pertain to hiring in Chapter 4 and also pick up some of those points around data in Chapter 5.

Conclusion

In this chapter, I have analysed the discourses that are shaping how the future of work is imagined. The sociotechnical imaginaries (Jasanoff, 2015) constructed in those books show how dominant discourses shape future visions and what remains unseen in these visions. By exploring how popular books discuss the future of work, it was possible to show how the debate is shaped by discussions around automation and augmentation (Kelan, 2023b; Raisch & Krakowski, 2021). I also highlighted some specific patterns related to gender. I have shown how visions of the future of work are meaningful in that they shape thinking of potential futures. In particular, I have shown how oppositional thinking and contrasting catastrophic futures with more utopians is a common strategy to focus attention on which futures are desirable. One rhetorical device to achieve that is to suggest that 'this time it is different'. While technologies have changed the job landscape for a long time, the argument regularly deployed in the books is that these changes are different to anything that we encountered before. Such a dystopia of the future of work is driven by oppositional thinking, in which man is pitched against machine in an epic battle. The man-against-machine trope refers to the risks of automation, where machines replace human labour, or in this imaginary scenario, more accurately men's labour. At the same time, some books stress that the future of work will also see augmentation where humans and machines collaborate. This collaboration between humans and machines has been called new diversity.

Men are constructed as particularly affected by the technology-induced changes in the workplace. While there is some concern for working-class men, the biggest area of concern are white-collar professionals. Those white-collar professionals appear generic, but as others have suggested (Cave, 2020), professional work is largely imagined as performed by men. That is in spite of the fact that women made inroads into those professions. The books also suggested that socio-emotional skills are a unique advantage of humans over machines. We will trace this pattern further in Chapter 3. Such socio-emotional skills are also required in those jobs that create human–machine interfaces. It was acknowledged that women are rare among the designers of technology. It was also suggested that looking at AI should include jobs in the wider AI supply chain, such as data labelling. We will take a closer look at this area in Chapter 5. Apart from a few examples of how technologies are gendered by design, gender and related diversity, topics were regularly discussed in relation to algorithmic bias, particularly in relation to hiring. We return to such questions in Chapter 4. This chapter has shown how popular books function as a first indicator for patterns in discourses on the future of work.

3

UNIQUELY HUMAN AND THE AUTOMATABILITY OF SOCIO-EMOTIONAL SKILLS

Introduction

In the Chapter 2, I have shown how in books on the future of work, socio-emotional skills are constructed as a core advantage of humans over machines. In this chapter, I want to explore this pattern of humans having an advantage over machines further. Specifically, I query in how far humans have indeed a core advantage over machines when it comes to emotions. In this chapter, I am also exploring in how far machines can read and train humans in relation to emotions. This is of particular relevance because who holds socio-emotional skills has long been gendered: socio-emotional skills are expected to reside in women but are rarely rewarded in women (Fletcher, 1999; Kelan, 2008a). This raises the question how these dynamics around socio-emotional skills play out in relation to digitalisation. It has also been argued that leaders need to display socio-emotional skills to empathise with those they lead (Fletcher, 2004). In fact, much training on diversity and inclusion tries to develop empathy in leaders (Kelan, 2023a). In this

DOI: 10.4324/9781003427100-3

chapter, I discuss how technologies allow for such training to be conducted in new formats such as in VR.

Whereas Chapter 2 focused on books that discuss the future of work, this chapter is based on the interviews (further details can be found in the appendix). In the interviews, I asked interviewees about changes that they perceive in relation to the future of work and technology and how they saw issues such as around automation and augmentation. The underlying material for the chapter is in nature very different to the books. Whereas the books presented carefully argued and evidenced ideas that had undergone normal book publishing processes, the interviews represent occasioned answers. While the answers were naturally less polished than text published in a book, they provided a particularly rich canvas to analyse discursive patterns that are regularly mobilised around the future of work, technology and gender. The answers often reflected the experiences of interviewees, including reflections on changes that they had perceived in the workplace. Some talked about new ways of working, whereas others discussed technologies they had developed. In some cases, I was able to try some of those technologies myself. I was thereby able to add an additional facet to the discussions through my own experience with these technologies.

This chapter thereby questions in how far socio-emotional skills are uniquely human and out of reach for machines. I first show how drudgework is expected to be automated because it follows repeatable patterns. I then outline which consequences this might have for task profiles and structures in professional work, before showing how socio-emotional skills are constructed as a competitive advantage for humans over machines. I then query if socio-emotional skills are uniquely human by showing how socio-emotional skills can be understood as patterns that can be automated. While it is technically possible to automate socio-emotional skills to a degree, such an automation of socio-emotional skills might not be deemed socially desirable.

Drudgework as Repeatable Patterns

A common theme in the interviews was to suggest that machines can do manual, repetitive and mundane tasks, which will free humans from the drudgery of work. Interestingly, drudgery harks back to one of the language roots of the word robot (Čapek, 1920; Oxford English Dictionary, 2023e) (see Chapter 1), although none of the interviewees made this connection.

In many ways, interviewees were less concerned about physical tasks being replaced. This might in part be due to the fact that physical labour being replaced is a common feature of discourses since the Industrial Revolution. There was a clear expectation that physical tasks could be easily done by machines. Lucy asserts that machines can easily do tasks that are purely based on physical power rather than human thought. It was discussed that technology could displace manual labour in assembly line work or factory type work. In contrast, interviewees were less concerned about work in warehouses being automated. Felicia, for instance, stated that these are workplaces where humans are treated like machines. Similarly, Myra talked about how warehouse workers are told by a bracelet what to do. For her, this means being treated as a human robot. What Felicia and Myra articulate is the fact that jobs being automated is not necessarily problematic because in many jobs, people are already treated like machines. In a sense, it is a continuation of automation that has been affecting largely jobs in manufacturing and warehouses. However, due to the quality of some of those jobs, particularly in warehouses, it was not considered as particularly problematic that these jobs might fall away.

Since I was mainly interested in professional work, most interviewees reflected on how professional work will change. Interviewees regularly referenced tasks that could be automated. In particular, interviewees focused on repetitive tasks that were singled out as ripe for automation in professional work. Prime targets for such automation are what William, who works in a law firm, called drudgework. He saw this drudgework as ready for automation. Interviewees like Yoshiro and Howard talked about how manual, repetitive and predictable tasks would be automated. Ralf mentions that these tasks might not be simple but can also be sophisticated, as long as they are based on repeatable patterns. If drudgework is disappearing, William suggested that humans can focus on higher-end and more interesting work. Peter describes this as people being able to focus on cognitive tasks that are more 'challenging, interesting and developmental'.

Another way to express this sentiment was to suggest that drudgework – or what Anastasia describes as boring work – takes away from creative tasks. A common example in architecture referred to how bathrooms are placed. Yoshiro recalls how in his early days in architecture, he was copying and pasting bathrooms into residential layouts – a task that he found dull and boring. This is no longer needed today. Anastasia similarly states that it is no longer required to draw mundane things like bathrooms and car parks because there is already a myriad of layouts available that one can use and adapt. In such contexts, it makes little sense to create 30 different layouts afresh. According to Yoshiro, patterns in architecture are well established. It is equally well established how a one-bedroom apartment should be structured, which means that there is no need to reinvent such spaces. The reason why such work is no longer needed is because as Yoshiro states architecture is based on patterns that are repeated over and over again. In order to automate tasks, these patterns have to be made explicit by transforming the knowledge from architects into rules that can be used to create algorithms. Caleb talks about the idea that architecture is about codifying aesthetics by creating a rule-based model that is predicting design options. These algorithms then encapsulate the knowledge, experience and the signature styles of architects, and the predictions such a system makes replicate a specific architectural style.

It is notable that other professional contexts brought up similar illustrations of automation. For instance, interviewees often reflected on how legal work changed through the years. Beverly comments that early in her career, she spent hours going through folders of documents with a pen, which is no longer done anymore. William similarly comments that lawyers no longer have to go through books because there are online legal databases they can use. Tessa talked about how lawyers use templates and have technology that changes clause numbers and definitions of a word automatically. In a bank context, Zac talks about the manual labour of putting numbers into spreadsheets, which is done automatically today. In auditing, Peter mentions that drones are checking stock in warehouses, meaning that auditors no longer have to travel to a location to make these checks physically. Duncan recalls how his organisation started to automate adding tax codes to long spreadsheets. These activities were normally done by junior accountants who went through two-thousand lines of a spreadsheet, adding tax codes manually. One could imagine that this work is rather tedious. When Duncan's organisation implemented technology for this task, he expected an uproar because the technology was taking away a huge chunk of the jobs that junior accountants were doing. However, Duncan recounts how the junior accountants were delighted that they no longer had to go through lines and lines of spreadsheet due to the tedious-ness of this task. Drudgework had been automated.

However, many of the interviewees also stated that such change in regard to technology is not new but forms part of changes that they have experienced in their lifetime. Victor, a consultant, said that consultants have been augmented by technology for a long time. He recalls how in the 1990s, Lotus Notes augmented the intelligence of consultants. Anastasia comments that in architecture, every new technology such as computer-aided design led to suggestions that architects will become redundant, and she sees the same arguments in relation to AI and machine learning. Beverly, a lawyer, mentioned that the 17 years of experience that she built up in her area of expertise have been replaced by generative AI. Beverly frames this as her expertise disappearing. Although one might presume that this is scary, Beverly seems less concerned about it. Overall, there was less panic about the changes in professional work in the interviews compared to the books. A common perspective was that while some jobs will disappear, others will appear. Anastasia articulates this as for every redundant job, there are 20 other new jobs emerging.

Shifting Tasks and Structures

It was widely acknowledged that tasks and structures of professional work might change. A common theme in the interviews was to talk about the changing tasks and structures in professional work. For instance, Yoshiro imagines that architects of the future will be 'shepherds of algorithms', which means that part of the professional task of the future will be to develop patterns that are coded. This constitutes a major change in regard to how architects do their work because a key part of the job will be to codify aesthetics into technology, to echo Caleb's earlier statement.

Other changes in the task profile refer, for instance, to how time is spent. Xerxes uses the example of how a programmer would traditionally need two hours to write a piece of code, but if the programmer uses ChatGPT, the same task can be done in five minutes. Victor talked about how man-agement consultants produce a lot of PowerPoint slides to communicate. In the past, he said that a consultant might spend 15 minutes to gather infor-mation and 45 minutes to 'massage' the slide to develop the right chart or graphic. That has now changed because consultants now spend the majority of time on deep thinking and the story that they want to tell; the creation of the slide itself is swift because there are automated tools that can be used. He maintains that the automation of slides will not make consultants redundant because the human is augmented but not replaced by technology.

Yet, Victor also acknowledges that there might be a time-saving component, which might in the long run affect the hourly pay structure that many professions employ. While Victor might have spent one hour to create a slide in the past, he would only require 30 minutes today and might create two slides instead of one in an hour. Yoshiro observes a similar time-saving component of technologies in architecture, where work that would have required four hours in the past can now be done in four minutes. Yet, clients are still charged for four hours. Beverly draws on a strikingly similar example, saying that work that would have taken a lawyer four hours to complete can now be completed in 30 seconds or less. She acknowledges that this will be a challenge to the normal charging structure by the hour that many professional firms use. If a task now only takes minutes, why would clients pay the high hourly rates of professionals? This questions the traditional hourly pay model employed in many professional firms.

New technologies also open up the possibility of changing how work is done. In particular, generative AI is seen as a game changer for professional work. Victor talks about how junior consultants use ChatGPT to bring themselves up to speed on specific client contexts swiftly. In the past, a consultant who is unfamiliar with how a bank operates might read Wikipedia and articles on financial blogs. Today, they will ask ChatGPT. Victor states that this will not make them an expert but it helps them to understand what a treasury department at a bank does. If the technology is a bit wrong about such basic information or even 'hallucinates', it does not matter greatly because it would not go into a report to the client but rather provides background knowledge to allow the consultants to understand a context swiftly. Victor is less concerned that management consulting could be replaced by generative AI because he likens the output of ChatGPT to how his teenage son would answer a question. It is a basic answer but lacks the level of sophistication and rigour that a client would pay 'big money' for.

In general, there were many examples of how ChatGPT and generative AI more generally are used in the professions. Anastasia talked about a marketing company that uses ChatGPT to generate pitch ideas and they then try to beat the system by coming up with better pitches. Beverly mentioned that in her law firm, they spent a lot of time on 'prompt engineering' to ensure that the responses from generative AI match what is required. William describes the use of generative AI as a creative sparring partner or a foil for creative thinking; it is used to develop ideas with a machine but it does not replace the human. Although generative AI might automate tasks in professional work, generative AI is mainly seen as a tool to condense information and to provide ideas, which augments professional work.

The time-saving component of technology can not only upend the charging structure in the professions but it might also require different organisational structures. Many professional firms are organised in a pyramid structure, where large numbers of junior professionals are hired and then compete to become one of the few partners. Victor talks about how there are thousands of young people in their 20s manually going through documents and circling items in Big Four firms – the largest professional service networks, namely Deloitte, EY, KPMG and PwC – when preparing taxes. Victor suggests that these thousands of young people might not be required in the future. Similarly, Beverly mentions that the pool of junior lawyers is going to be shrinking as a consequence of drudgework no longer being required to the same degree.

There was also a sentiment that if junior professionals no longer have to do drudgework, they miss out on learning. Victor talks about how early in his career, a lot of learning came through doing boring stuff, which allowed him to build up mental 'muscle memory'. He describes 'muscle memory' as a reflex to know what might be wrong in a situation. Caleb talks about a similar moment in regard to architecture, where the experience of having confronted a problem in a previous situation helps architects to solve a current problem. Yoshiro also mentions how architectural patterns became for him second nature through repetition and working closely with other architects. While it was common to see drudgework as a form of learning, which might no longer be possible, Anastasia presumed that technology can in fact help junior architects to develop knowledge to do the job well. She argues that technology can assist junior architects in building what she calls an intuition. Such an intuition would in her view take years to cultivate otherwise. In a sense, she argues that the intuition developed through drudgework can be replaced by the coded experience in technology.

Professional work is often based on an apprenticeship model where junior people learn by observing others. William calls this osmotic learning.

According to Victor, it is not just doing manual tasks over and over again that constitutes learning in the professions, but also sitting in thousand conference rooms to understand what makes different executives tick. Various interviewees talked about how much time junior lawyers spent observing more senior lawyers to see how they deal with clients and how to tackle specific issues. A traditional argument is that if more tasks are automated, reducing the need for junior lawyers, they will have less chance to observe how to do their jobs once they become more senior. In many ways, the pandemic provided a glimpse at some of the problems that the lack of shadowing senior colleagues might have in the future. Due to the fact that work was done remotely, many junior lawyers missed out on the opportunity to observe the day-to-day requirements of what it means to be a senior lawyer. Tessa explained this as follows: whereas before, junior lawyers would sit close to a senior lawyer and overhear how the senior lawyer takes urgent client calls, during the pandemic, the junior lawyers were often not included in ad hoc client meetings because the client either called on a mobile or the video meeting link was not circulated to the junior lawyers. Before, junior lawyers would soak up knowledge through observation; they were now excluded from such processes because they were no longer physically present in the space. William talks about how even arranging a debrief after an online meeting with a client has the additional hurdle of setting up another online meeting. If, structurally, much of the repeatable tasks are done by machines, leading to fewer junior professionals being required, this could mean that the progression from junior to senior professional and the entire structure of professional firms might need to change.

There are also wider changes to the professions that the interviewees imagined. For instance, Beverly likened the changes in the legal profession to the reformation where people get access to something that was previously closely guarded. She describes this as a democratisation of legal knowledge, which in her view is a positive development. Yoshiro echoes this point when he suggests that due to professionalisation, knowledge became protected and a charge is due to access this knowledge; for instance, consultants are charging for their knowledge and knowledge is sitting behind paywalls. He argues that technology means that such knowledge could be accessed differently. He suggests that making such knowledge – which in his view lies in patterns in architecture – more widely accessible would be beneficial. There might also be benefits for smaller firms, as Anastasia hinted when suggesting that technology can level the playing field to allow smaller architectural practices to compete with larger ones. Overall, these changes in tasks and structures suggest that what humans might do in the future of work changes. I will trace this in the next section.

The Human Advantage

We have seen so far that in professional work, drudgework is seen as automatable, and while that brings certain challenges for tasks and structures, the overall sentiment in the interviews was that technology is augmenting work. Viewing these changes more holistically, some interviewees commented how automating drudgework would allow people to spend their time differently. Jeffrey likened this emerging future as akin to Star Trek, the sci-fi franchise; Jeffrey suggests that in Star Trek, humans can dedicate themselves to exploration and creation, which in a sense would free individuals to engage in other activities. Gabrielle said automation will free up time for humans to do other things, which, as she points out, might not only relate to the public sphere of work but also entail other activities like caring for family members.

Most thinking on what humans might do centred on the idea what machines currently cannot do, or where the use of machines would be undesirable. Those areas largely required social interaction. For instance, Ralf suggested that anything that works based on relationships, such as sales or customer service, will require humans. Bank tellers are a profession that is often mentioned in relation to technological change. For instance, Bessen (2015) discusses the assumption that with the introduction of ATMs, bank tellers might disappear. However, rather than disappearing, the tasks that bank tellers engaged in changed (Bessen, 2015). Similarly, Oscar, who works in a bank, references bank tellers because their jobs are seen as under threat by digitalisation. However, Oscar was of the opinion that much of the work that bank tellers would have traditionally done in a branch would in the future be moving to the back office. Bank tellers would likely be dealing with similar issues as today, but the interaction is facilitated by digital technologies. This speaks to the point that personal relationships will require a human touch. Jeffrey talked about other areas where human input would be required, such as in bereavement counselling. Rather than HR sending an automated message, he would expect that a human conversation is required in such situations. Kenneth also talks about empathy that is, for instance, shown in healthcare as being hard to replace. In a similar vein, Ben suggests that since tasks that can be done by a machine will be done by a machine in the future, this leaves soft skills to humans. This includes understanding and managing the self and others. Ben presumes that humans will be in demand for those soft skills.

It is perhaps not surprising that socio-emotional skills are singled out as particularly important in regard to professional work. For instance, Victor talks about the importance of 'reading the room' for a consultant. A consultant presenting to a client will notice if the CEO is nodding but other executives are sceptical. A consultant would then know to schedule extra meetings with the sceptical executives to bring them on board. He suggests that technology cannot do this inter-human work. Similarly, Victor talks about the importance of executive assistants who he describes as the social glue. While many of the tasks that executive assistants do, such as scheduling meetings, could be automated, executive assistants do much more than this: they know what is happening in the office, they know the politics and they read every email, which gives them additional social knowledge that a machine could not replicate, according to Victor.

This also has consequences on how professional firms are likely to hire in the future. Beverly reflected about what type of people a future law firm might need to recruit. She suggests that in the future, law firms need people who are better at listening to clients. Beverly acknowledges that generative AI can provide many answers but that a lawyer has to understand the client. The lawyer needs to understand if the client is more risk-averse or open to risk, which will inform the legal strategy suggested. She says that as a managing partner in a legal firm, she would be looking to recruit individuals with listening skills, or what she calls an 'emphatic lawyer'. The notion of the empathic lawyer encapsulates the idea that socio-emotional skills are constructed as vital in the future of work. In a similar vein, William talks about how working with clients requires an understanding of the culture and the power dynamics in the organisation. He talks about how an experienced lawyer has to understand the culture and the power dynamics that happen in this context, which is used to solve problems and find a consensus. This is not legal knowledge as such but what he describes as tacit knowledge that people have akin to a gut feeling or an intuition.

The overall idea that emerges from the interviews is that if parts of professional work are automated, then socio-emotional skills become a competitive advantage of humans. This is largely to the fact that socio-emotional skills are constructed as uniquely human. In other words, those skills either cannot be performed by machines or it is socially not desirable that those skills are performed by machines. By focusing on socio-emotional skills as uniquely human, the interviewees also suggest that machines will not replace human labour completely. The interview accounts were, by and large, hopeful. Drudgework is handed over to machines and humans can focus on interesting work, and work that requires socio-emotional skills. It is here that humans shine because they can do things that machines are perceived as unable to do or where the use of machines is undesirable.

The Gendering of Socio-Emotional Skills

Traditionally, discussions about socio-emotional skills were gendered. Stereotypically, it is presumed that women are particularly good at and well-suited for displaying socio-emotional skills. Such ideas are, for instance, drawn upon by CEOs, who justify gender equality by referring to such gender essentialised skills (Kelan & Wratil, 2021). These stereotypes have consequences in the workplace in that women displaying socio-emotional skills are often not rewarded for them; the assumption is that women simply do what comes naturally to them (Fletcher, 1999; Kelan, 2008a). Yet, in the interviews like in the books, those socio-emotional skills were rarely gendered. The only example of a person linking socio-emotional skills with gender came from Duncan. Duncan argues that women should find it easier to stay employed when automation takes hold. He admits that he has no specific data for this assumption but in his observation of 20 years, he noticed that women are better than men at persuading people to adopt their ideas and at building teams and communities, which is central in professional services jobs. Duncan here establishes a link between gender and skills in that he argues that women are better at building teams and persuading others. He suggests that these socio-emotional skills might give women the edge when it comes to skills required in the workplace.

Socio-emotional skills were loosely linked to gender in relation to care work. Gabrielle talked about how with an ageing population, there is increased demand for healthcare workers. Since women are over-presented in healthcare jobs, she saw that as an opportunity to grow a care economy, which in turn would give women better jobs prospects. In a similar vein, Felicia argues that care jobs are not threatened by automation and, because women tend to be in care professions, they have future sources of employment. Tina talked about how jobs in which women are concentrated are less likely to be automated, such as those involving care. This for her included caring for children, older persons and working in healthcare. In these cases, socio-emotional skills were linked to women through care work and discursively used to suggest that women might find it easier to be employed in the future. In general, it is interesting to note that socio-emotional skills were rarely discussed as gendered in the books on the future of work and in the interviews. This is a departure from earlier research, which has shown a strong stereotypical connection between socio-emotional skills and women. In the few instances when socio-emotional skills were linked to women, in all of those cases, socio-emotional skills were constructed as skills for the future and there was a suggestion that these changes might be beneficial for women.

Care as Automatable

In general, paid care work was regularly constructed as an area that provides secure employment in the future. This shone through in some of the interviews and in one of the books I analysed. Yet, when care and automation was discussed, one particular example came up several times: PARO. The PARO seal is a white cuddly toy robot, taking the shape of a seal. It is created by the Japanese National Institute of Advanced Industrial Science and Technology (AIST). PARO is a therapeutic robot that can interact with humans through sensors that measure temperature, light, touch, voice and posture (PARO, 2023). It is deployed in care homes and in working with dementia patients. It was notable that four of the interviewees brought up PARO unprompted.

Jeffrey tells me about a common occurrence when he talks about technology in the world of work at conferences. Inevitably, someone in the audience will state that technology could not be used in care work or in hospitality. His standard response is that it is happening already, citing the example of the PARO seal.[1] He suggests that AI is already used for socio-emotional work like in care and describes the fluffy seal as an example of that. Jeffrey here used the PARO seal to challenge the idea that care work cannot be automated. As such, PARO is discursively used to suggest that a machine can replace socio-emotional skills. Kenneth, another interviewee, also uses the example of how AI, in this case, PARO, is used in Japanese care homes. Kenneth draws on this example to illustrate that empathy-like behaviour is not out of reach for machines.

Tina and Felicia invoke PARO in slightly different ways to Kenneth and Jeffrey. Tina talks about a fluffy seal pup used in Japan to work with Alzheimer's patients and suggests that it has a remarkable effect. This implies that the technology is employed in such a way that benefits patients. Similarly, Felicia talked about a 'little baby seal' for the use of dementia patients. However, Felicia stresses that this supposed automation of care work only succeeds if a trained caregiver is initiating the interaction, such as, handing PARO to a patient. Rather than replacing care workers, PARO augments them. This chimes with results from research that shows that PARO automates care only to a specific extent, because most interactions with the robot seal have to be initiated by carers (Chevallier, 2023).

These examples illustrate how emblematic PARO has become for discussing technology and socio-emotional skills. PARO can be used to challenge the idea that socio-emotional skills are uniquely human. In fact, PARO can function as an example that socio-emotional can be automated and augmented by technology. This example also fractures the discourse that socio-emotional skills are uniquely human, and as such, the core advantage that humans bring to the table in the future of work. I want to trace this idea further by looking at instances where machines perform socio-emotional skills.

Machines and Socio-Emotional Skills

The common consensus in the interviews and also in the books on the future of work was that socio-emotional skills are a competitive advantage of humans and cannot be automated. However, one interviewee, Kenneth, in particular, questioned in how far work that requires human emotions might be safe from automation. Kenneth expressed this through using the word empathy. Kenneth states that researchers who argue that jobs that require empathy are safe from automation because computers do not have empathy and are simultaneously 'right and wrong'. He justifies his thinking, which differs significantly from other interviewees, by saying that machines are reading human emotions such as facial expressions and body language – he suggests that with enough training data, a machine can figure out that if someone yawns, the person is bored. Kenneth says that a machine does not need empathy to figure that out – just enough training data on how humans react when they are bored. He describes empathy as an AI training challenge, and references Soul Machines and a digital human who is called Lia, who can 'recognise your emotions' and reflects them back as you.

I have subsequently tested a demo from Soul Machines that was available on their website. Instead of Lia, I meet Viola. Viola is an African American woman. When engaging with her, I was rather fascinated by the fact that a lot of design attention must have gone into creating her. I was impressed that she moved her face while talking like a human would do, including blinking her eyes and wrinkling her forehead when speaking. I tried to move my face in different ways and I had the impression that Viola was indeed at least in part mirroring my own facial expressions. Even though Viola's facial expressions were surprisingly realistic, it was nevertheless obvious that Viola is not a real person. In regard to holding a conversation, Viola can answer only fairly simple questions like how, why and when. To answer those questions, I am offered references from the internet, YouTube videos or other keywords that I could be interested in. With more complicated questions, Viola struggles. Yet, such technology mirrors human facial expressions and as such, mimics what could be described as socio-emotional skills.

Kenneth expands on his idea that socio-emotional skills can be automated by stressing that machines are able to read verbal and non-verbal communication and formulate appropriate responses. Through web cameras, machines can pick up heart rates, they can evaluate the tone of voice, the vocabulary one uses or can predict if a person has a heart attack. Machines can – at least according to Kenneth – even tell based on eye movement if you are lying. Kenneth was clearly questioning the commonly held assumption that jobs that require emotions are firmly in the realm of humans. He suggests that any jobs that require empathy and compassion, but also other emotions like anger and aggression, machines will be able to do. In fact, he argues that machines will even be able to pick up small facial movements that other humans might miss. Kenneth goes as far to suggest that machines might be the 'better empathetic entity' than actual people in the future.

What Kenneth presents here is a future where machines read and mimic human emotions, which will allow them to do many jobs that were done by humans before. My own engagement with Viola clearly shows the limitations of such technologies, but techno-enthusiasts might argue that these technologies will improve over time. Equally, there are many jobs around caring that a machine will struggle to perform, and Kenneth himself argues that healthcare will be difficult to automate. However, one can see how such technologies can be used in anything from customer service to hiring. I am particularly interested in the alternative vision of the future that Kenneth puts forward. Whereas socio-emotional skills were constructed as firmly in the hands of humans, Kenneth offers an alternative account here where machines are able to perform emotional work and can take this work over, too, eroding the competitive advantage that is attributed to humans.

Machines Training and Assessing Socio-Emotional Skills

In order to trace how socio-emotional skills could be performed by machines, it is useful to turn first to the hiring context, where socio-emotional skills are regularly assessed (a fuller review of technology in hiring will follow in Chapter 4). Anton worked in an organisation that created technological solutions for hiring. He talked about how the technology they design in his company assesses emotions. He outlines that one first has to define which socio-emotional skills one is looking for. The company also defines communication parameters such as if the person can be understood easily, speed of speech and intelligibility. For instance, if one wishes to assess empathy, one might define that a person should talk about others rather than only herself. This, according to Anton, is a way to assess empathy. After these basic elements are defined, the software will emulate daily interactions. To illustrate the point, Anton provides an example of how a co-worker or customer approaches the candidate with an issue to be solved. The candidate then interacts with this other person and is evaluated based on how well the previously defined characteristics are met. In this case, a machine is evaluating the performance of socio-emotional skills.

This approach of first defining what is important in any given situation in regard to emotional response and then comparing this to the actual performance in the situation was common for assessment and training providers. Kenneth gives an example of how AI is being used to coach and train individuals. He uses the example of call centre workers, who are trained to be empathetic and compassionate. Kenneth terms this a coaching augmentation and a learning augmentation, where the technology is used to develop human competencies, specifically in regard to socio-emotional skills.

As part of the research for this book, I tested various technologies that are designed to train people in VR. In one example, I was a grocery store worker. In the VR, my task was to up-sell customers by engaging them on a human level. When I looked around my virtual environment, I saw a typical grocery store environment. A simulated customer appears. The customer looks artificial, like most of the characters I met in the simulations. The customer has a shopping cart[2] in front of her and I notice that she has baking ingredients. I recognise the baking ingredients: they are what is needed for American chocolate chip cookies. I remember my task: to sell her something in addition to what she already has. I am given a choice of specific questions that appear on my screen. I have to click and select one to progress. The options included, among others, 'Are you looking for something?', 'How is your day going?' and 'What is for dessert?' I pick the last question, which appears like a good choice because, as I am told, it is an open question, allowing me to engage with the customer. My simulated customer responds that she will be baking chocolate chip cookies but 'wants to mix it up'. This is apparently my window to up-sell her by suggesting additional ingredients. As feedback, the app tells me that I did well by looking at the shopping cart. I remember being surprised at the fact that the technology noticed this. I presume that it either checked my head movement or my eye movement to come to this assessment. At first, I feel like I was caught in the act, as if my private thoughts had been exposed. I do remember that I had looked at the cart and concluded that the person is planning to bake chocolate chip cookies. For this, I drew on my experience of baking such chocolate chip cookies while living in the United States. Someone who did not have this experience would probably not know how these ingredients are used. This knowledge helped me to pass the exercise. If I had not known what the ingredients are for, I might have learned about them in the process of doing the exercise, which then would help me in real life to understand how I can up-sell a customer. What was, however, deeply memorable is having this feeling of being caught in the act when the VR pointed out that I had looked at the cart.

However, such accurate assessments were the exception rather than the rule. In most cases, I was frustrated by the fact that the technology did not understand me well enough. During one of the VR experiences, I remember addressing the characters in a conflict situation by their first name to ensure that they felt heard. When I was asked to record short responses, I used the first names of the individuals. Yet, the feedback I got was that I should use first names more often. Since using first names more often would have been overusing this technique, I concluded that the technology did not understand me well enough to note that I had used first names. The first names, such as 'Sarah', were provided to the technology as keywords to look for. If the candidate uses 'Sarah', then the candidate is evaluated positively. However, I noticed that very often when I used 'Sarah', the technology would not register this. The feedback that I should use first names more often is of course less useful if I recall using 'Sarah' several times, but the technology simply did not understand and register this.

This was not an isolated experience but rather common across lots of different platforms. In another case, I was a mental health worker visiting a depressed and suicidal person at her home. My task was to show empathy for her situation and to offer some strategies she can employ to feel better. In the simulation, I suggested that the person should 'prepare a simple meal'. Yet, I got the feedback that I should have suggested to her to 'cook'. In this case, the words 'cook' and 'cooking' had been used in the design of the technology. The words 'prepare a simple meal' had not been entered a keyword. I remember feeling frustrated that the technology was not assessing me correctly because I used different words that were not programmed as part of the keywords.

In another scenario, I was learning how to give better presentations. When I had similar training before, I was told to avoid filler words and I remember learning about techniques to avoid such filler words. Yet, to my surprise, I discovered that the technology presumed it was good to use filler words: I got the feedback to use more filler words. What this example illustrates is that different expectations of what constitutes a good presentation technique are employed and coded in technology. In this case, what constitutes good speech was to use filler words. I also got feedback on the pace of speech, hand gestures and eye contact. Eye contact was a rather tricky one. I found looking into the eyes of many of the avatars was a rather strange experience. One clearly notes that the avatars are not real, and it feels odd to look them in the eyes. Based on that feedback of a lack of eye contact, I decided to stare at the avatars' eyes. In a real-life interaction I am sure my staring eye contact would have been perceived negatively. Yet when I stared, I still got the feedback that I do not make enough eye contact. I wondered in how far the technology tracking me might not be as accurately calibrated as it should be.

Rather than analysing the context of talk, the feedback I received in VR was purely on the delivery of the talk. In another situation, I got additional feedback that I need to look more to the right or the left. One of my favourites was a unique score that I got in some of the exercises. This unique score, as the app told me, was measuring if an 11-year-old would understand me. I found this to be a rather odd metric because all the trainings were designed to be in professional work contexts rather than schools, and as such, the interaction with 11-year-olds might be rather limited. I also wondered how the score came about. Had people been recorded before and an 11-year-old had listened to the recording to check comprehension?

As such, the feedback that such apps provide was in my experience rather mixed. Some of it was helpful, whereas other things kept coming up even when I did specifically that in the next reiteration. Much of this technology is still in infancy and feedback will likely get better over the years. I also wondered in how far such technologies could be reliably chosen, for instance, to select candidates. If the technology does not understand me, I am sure that other people with accents would also struggle. If the technology could not track my eye movement accurately, I am not sure if I would be selected for a job that requires such a connection.

Hands as Liminal in VR

VR training is designed to transport the learners into a new space where they can practice new skills. Immersion is thus key. One common assumption is that immersion requires a highly realistic scenario where simulated people appear real. For all VR apps I used, that was far from being the case. As I mentioned before, it was clear to me that the avatars I interacted with are not real people. Their eyes would often look particularly weird and they lacked any facial expression that I valued, for instance, with Viola, the technology from Soul Machines that I tried. Viola only appeared on my computer screen rather than in VR. However, it was notable that in VR environments, efforts had been made to give the avatars different voices by those who created them, and I appreciated that some characters had accents that sounded either French or African. Although attempts had been made to make the scenarios realistic, initially, I thought it would be hard to imagine that one can immerse oneself in the environment.

Others I spoke to had similar concerns. Franklin, for instance, recounts a story of how one of the participants of a VR training was highly resistant to undergo health and safety training in this new format. He tried to convince his colleagues that they should all refuse this training. However, he could be persuaded to give it a go. He put the headset on and started the simulation. At one point, he flinched – in the VR scenario, a nail had gone through his hand. Even though this person had been sceptical about the training, having the experience of a nail going through his hand shocked him. He realises that what the training offers is something more than a theoretical understanding of what can happen if you do not adhere to health and safety standards. Franklin describes this an 'emotional impact' in the interview where the nail-through-the-hand scenario created additional learning that at least according to Franklin is difficult to achieve in another way.

While doing VR training myself, I was regularly invited to pick an avatar. On most platforms, I could select from a set of preset characters. There are commonly less modification options than I had experienced building an avatar for one of the virtual recruitment events I attended, where one had a lot of choice in how one presents oneself, including the ability to wear flip-flops in recruitment simulations. In VR, however, it seemed more common to pick an avatar that was pre-established. There was less of a temptation to build an avatar that might correspond more closely to how you might appear in real life. Instead, I was offered the option to appear as a Latino or a Black woman. In most cases, I forgot which avatar I had picked because it was fairly inconsequential for most of the VR interactions I engaged in. Yet, at several times during the experience, I was shocked when my hands looked different in VR than in real life. I noted in my field notes that I was surprised when my finger nails had bright red nail polish on.

Together with the example that Franklin recounted earlier, it appears that hands occupy a liminal space between the physical and the virtual world. During a VR experience, you not only have a headset on that blocks out the physical environment in which you are situated and replaces it with a virtual environment, but you also hold controllers in your hands, which allow you to drive the action by clicking on certain elements. As a matter of fact, during the initial familiarisation with VR, I learned how to manipulate virtual objects by using the controller. For instance, I would learn to lift an object and then throw it. Your hand movement is also used in some metrics to analyse, for example, your body language. If you cross your arms, the controllers will also be crossed, which is read as a closed body position. While in other VR environments, the body moves around more dynamically, in most of the training in VR I completed, I was stationary, either standing or sitting, but rarely moving through space. Glancing at my hands in VR was thus one of the few instances where it became clear that my embodiment as a virtual avatar was different. This often led to a moment of surprise akin to what the person who had a nail go through his virtual hand must have experienced.

My VR experiences did not include a nail-through-the-hand scenario like Franklin describes, but it is not hard to imagine based on my own experiences that there is a moment of shock and surprise. The hands seem to be liminal boundary between a sense of self as a person and the virtual environment in which one finds oneself.

Perspective Taking

Apart from health and safety applications, VR was presented as particularly useful to help humans to practise socio-emotional skills that are constructed as important for the future of work. Matt expressed this by referencing what he calls an 'old adage', that one must walk a mile in someone else's shoes to comprehend their life situation. He explains that this is particularly useful for diversity and inclusion because VR allows you to try on someone else's shoes. VR allows you to take someone else's place and make an experience that you might normally not have. Matt provides the example of taking on the position of a woman colleague and play through a scenario from her perspective. Matt argues that this helps with taking perspective and is more impactful than watching a video. He says that by being in VR in this situation, you might 'feel your blood boil' because you are treated unfairly. This suggests that VR allows access to emotions that one normally might not experience, which in turn can help to develop empathy for others.

Franklin offered another strikingly similar explanation as to why VR works well in regard to diversity and inclusion training. Franklin describes how VR training allows you to experience what it feels like to be marginalised. He argues that for many people who did not have such experiences before, it is tricky to understand what marginalisation feels like. This is said to limit their potential to take action on it. Franklin suggests that VR training gets people over the hurdle to understand what it feels like to be in such a situation and how to respond to that. He likens it to the difference between an academic explanation and the practical experience. For Franklin, if you experience being the odd person out or that your ideas are not appreciated, people develop what he calls their soft skills. What we see here is that technology is used to allow people to make different experiences to develop socio-emotional skills.

In regard to how such training is delivered, I had the opportunity to participate in several diversity and inclusion trainings in VR. In one scenario, I met Steve, who treated Sandra in sexist ways. One of the exercises involved pressing the controller in my left hand for inclusive behaviours and the controller in the right for exclusive behaviours. Following this, I was presented with a range of sentences I could pick from to advance the conversation. Depending on my choice, I was given feedback if that was a good or bad choice. One element I noticed is that when I talked with Steve, he seemed to mirror my behaviour – if I was aggressive, he also became aggressive. This mirroring is what actors who are engaged to perform diversity and inclusion scenarios in person have also been asked to do. I did not expect this to be a feature of the VR training. The key learning of the training was to allow Steve to come up with why his behaviour is problematic himself rather than telling him what was wrong.

The final part of the scenario involved me recording a closing statement in which I addressed Steve directly and outlined what we had agreed in terms of the way forward. Then I changed avatar and was in Steve's position. I saw the avatar that I had chosen before deliver the speech that had just recorded back to me. As Steve, I would notice how it felt to be at the receiving end of such messages. I could then shift back and re-record the message. The idea was that I notice myself that something was too harsh or not clear and that I could then correct that in the next reiteration. This form of self-feedback was rather useful. Such retakes are not possible in real life and are tedious in physical training, but they are a key feature of VR. I can practise as much as I want. It obviously relies on the trainee to spot things that do not work well.

Role plays and other theatre-based methods are regularly employed in diversity and inclusion training, often making use of actors or putting employees in different roles. They can be rather effective for perspective taking. However, VR allows for this to be elevated. Rather than enacting a situation with a colleague or an actor, which is artificial in itself, VR allows participants to engage in such exercises on their own. Seeing the world from a different vantage point can be facilitated by VR. This is essential to develop empathy and the socio-emotional skills that are constructed as the human core advantage. Yet such training is delivered by a machine. Of course, humans design the technologies, but the actual training of socio-emotional skills is machine-facilitated. Machines are thus able to train socio-emotional skills in humans, complicating the idea that socio-emotional skills are out of reach of machines.

Socio-Emotional Skills as Patterns

So far, I have shown that machines are able to mimic and train humans in socio-emotional skills. Since socio-emotional skills follow repeatable patterns, socio-emotional skills can be automated. Like many of the repeatable patterns that can be automated in spreadsheets, legal documents or presentation slides, socio-emotional skills follow patterns that can be transferred into code. Such processes of transferring emotions into computer patterns are subjective, and how subjective assessments are transformed into objective and universal assessments will be at the centre of Chapter 5. While these processes are deeply problematic, for the purpose of this chapter, the fact that socio-emotional patterns can be automated casts doubt on the construction of socio-emotional skills as uniquely human, and as such, as a core competitive advantage of humans over machines.

If and to what degree socio-emotional skills will be automated depends also on what is deemed socially acceptable. For example, it has been shown that having machines involved in childcare is technically possible but is deemed by experts in the field as problematic for social reasons due to implications for children's development and privacy concerns (Lehdonvirta et al., 2023). Therefore, it is possible that socio-emotional skills at work will continue to be completed by humans. However, this might not be due to the fact that socio-emotional skills cannot be performed by machines but rather due to a desire to have humans perform those skills.

However, there is potential to use technology to train individuals. For instance, the empathetic professional, to paraphrase Beverly, might well be trained by machines to understand how to better support colleagues and clients. If the patterns that constitute drudgework can be embedded in machines to give professionals a substrate of the experience of many years of professional practice, then this is certainly possible in relation to socio-emotional skills as well. When Anastasia talked about how technology might provide junior professionals with an intuition that is trained on previous patterns and thus provides access to professional experience, this intuition might also extend to how to display socio-emotional skills.

Conclusion

In this chapter, I questioned in how far socio-emotional skills are a core human advantage for humans over machines. I illustrated that most interviewees expected drudgework that follows repeatable patterns to be completed by machines in the future. In professional work, this meant, for instance, that individuals would no longer go manually through long documents but that technology could do that work. It also involved using technology to learn and to create outputs. If parts of professional work are automated, this changes the task profile of professionals and is likely having an impact on how professional firms are structured. In particular, this might affect the need for large groups of junior people who engage in much of the drudgework. However, rather than seeing the professions as disappearing as a consequence, interviewees talked about how this might democratise professional knowledge by making it more widely available. It was also stressed that professionals will require a different skill set, such as being empathetic. It is interesting to note that like most of the books, the interviewees largely resisted the idea to construct socio-emotional skills as something women are good at. This constitutes a departure to how socio-emotional skills are often talked about.

Empathy, as well as other socio-emotional skills, were regularly constructed as uniquely human and thus out of reach of machines. In this chapter, I questioned in how far socio-emotional skills are indeed outside of the reach of machines and thus constitute a human advantage. I first looked at how interviewees talked about care work and automation to then focus on how machines emulate emotions or train emotional responses, including in VR. I have suggested that even though the experiences in VR appear artificial, they might be well-suited to develop socio-emotional skills in participants. The future empathetic professional might well be trained in VR. The chapter questioned if socio-emotional skills are uniquely human and as such constitute the core competitive advantage of humans over machines. However, while socio-emotional skills are automatable to a degree, it is questionable if this is socially desirable.

Notes

1 As a side note, when Jeffrey and I spoke, it was during one of the Covid lockdowns and schools were closed. While Jeffrey was speaking with me, his daughter was sitting at the same table doing the work the school had given her but also listening in on the interview. Jeffrey could not remember the name of the seal and only after his daughter searched for it online, she reminds him that it is called PARO.
2 I use shopping cart and cookies here because the VR experience was situated in the United States.

4

ALGORITHMIC BIAS AS ULTIMATELY FIXABLE

Introduction

Finding people with the right skills to do jobs is centrally important for organisations to function well. Hiring also often follows specific patterns such as identifying skills that are needed in different functions in the organisation. Yet hiring is complex and time-consuming, making hiring an ideal area to deploy technology. One cannot fail to see how for an organisation, it must be appealing to use technology to determine which candidate is best suited for a role. In many ways, using technology to recruit people follows the idea that something as perceived subjective as hiring can be transformed into an objective process (Kang, 2023). However, the processes through which this presumed objectivity is achieved are far from unproblematic (Kang, 2023). Technology also has the potential to help with another aspect of the hiring process: the bias of those who select the candidate. For a long time, recruitment has been impacted by human bias and technology offers the possibility to reduce this bias (Feloni, 2017; McIlvaine, 2018; Riley,

DOI: 10.4324/9781003427100-4

2018). Therefore, AI in hiring is a techno-optimist's dream in that processes of an organisation are improved through technology.

However, this techno-optimism is in many ways dampened by the fact that AI has been shown to repeat and amplify bias in hiring (Dalenberg, 2018; Vassilopoulou et al., 2024; Kelan, 2024). The media is regularly pointing to dangers associated with AI in hiring. Amazon's failed attempt to use AI in hiring functions is the standard example used in the media (BBC News, 2018; Dastin, 2018) and beyond. In this case, the pattern that the AI identified and repeated through predictions was exclusionary. If AI is amplifying biases then this raises serious questions if using AI in hiring can indeed fulfil this techno-optimistic dream. In this chapter, I question how a techno-optimist's stance that entails that AI improves business processes can be reconciled with the existence of algorithmic bias in hiring. I suggest that this is achieved by constructing algorithmic bias as ultimately fixable. Techno-optimism as a stance was supplemented with the perspective of techno-hesitation. Techno-hesitation is not a rejection of technology as such. A rejection of technology or an acknowledgement that technology can lead to more harm than good would be akin to the stance of techno-pessimism. Instead, this stance presents a hesitation that could be dissolved once there is more societal acceptance of and confidence in the use of AI in hiring.

Hiring the Candidates that Best Meet the Profile

Although all parts of human resources can potentially be impacted by digitalisation (Cheng & Hackett, 2021; Tambe et al., 2019), hiring has been an area at the forefront of being transformed through digital processes (Eubanks, B., 2018). Reasons why hiring is a prime candidate for digitalisation are due to the repetitive nature of the process and the potential reduction of mistakes that digitalisation offers (Eubanks, B., 2018). In addition, digitalisation can broaden the candidate pool, make the hiring process more efficient, lead to higher job tenure, and make the process quicker and reduce costs (Black & van Esch, 2020; Hoffman et al., 2015; Johnson et al., 2021; Tippins et al., 2021).

Digitalisation can be used in a range of processes in the hiring funnel (Sánchez-Monedero & Dencik, 2019; Sánchez-Monedero et al. 2020). However, there are certain aspects in the hiring process where the use of digital technologies is more common, such as screening candidates (Albert, 2019). For instance, a candidate might join a virtual careers fair to meet an employer. Before submitting an application, the candidate can be invited to engage with a chatbot to check if basic requirements for the job are met. If so, the candidate might be invited to submit a CV, which is then checked based on certain keywords. It has been noted that some candidates attempt to game the system by, for instance, submitting a CV that includes references to elite universities like Oxford and Cambridge in white text that is invisible to the human eye but that would be picked up if an AI searched for keywords that include such elite universities (Buranyi, 2018). If a candidate's CV is selected, candidates might then be invited to participate in a number of simulations and games to test their skills and abilities (Tippins, 2015). In case candidates proceed further, they are commonly asked to participate in asynchronous online interviews where candidates might use a mobile phone or computer to record themselves answering a series of questions designed to see if the candidates are a good fit for the position (Köchling & Wehner, 2020; Albert, 2019).

The hiring process is expected to be changed significantly by digitalisation, but many of the underlying principles of hiring will apply to digitalised forms of hiring as much as they do to non-digitalised forms of hiring. Human resource practitioners often rely on guidelines such as the 'Uniform Guidelines On Employee Selection Procedures' (Biddle Consulting Group, 2023) to guide the hiring process. Before starting a hiring process, a job analysis is commonly conducted in which knowledge, skills, abilities and other characteristics (KSAOs) are identified that are required to do the job well. Then assessments are developed that assess the candidates against the KSAOs. This is ensured through a variety of validity tests that are conducted. These entail criterion-validity or, in other words, that the selection procedure predicts job performance; content validity, which means that what is being assessed is indicative of doing the job well; finally, construct validity, which shows that the data collection is indicative of how well the KSAOs are matched by the candidate (Biddle Consulting Group, 2023).

If hiring is digitalised, a similar process should be followed, apart from the fact that technology is more central in it. Historically, a candidate might have been invited to complete a pen-and-paper assessment, which is evaluated by humans for fit with KSAOs. Now, candidates might be invited to complete various games online to assess to what degree candidates fulfil the KSAOs. This means that how data is collected as part of candidate assessments is now digital. Data for such an assessment can come from a variety of sources. Data on work experience and educational background normally comes from CVs that are screened and then evaluated. CVs are commonly entered into applicant tracking systems (ATS). ATS are used by 98% of Fortune 500 companies to screen for keywords, leading to around 75% of candidates being rejected (*The Economist*, 2018; Sánchez-Monedero et al. 2020). The keywords used should emerge through the job analysis and be related to the KSAOs (Tippins, 2015; Johnson et al., 2021). If the candidate progresses, online tests and games provide further data points to assess the suitability of the candidates and again should measure the KSAOs. Other data sources include recorded asynchronous video interviews that are then evaluated against the KSAOs. Since the aim of the process is to evaluate how good a candidate's fit is with the KSAOs, digitalisation becomes visible in how this achieved: data is fed into algorithms, weighted and statistically analysed to then make a prediction about how well the respective candidate measures up against the KSAOs or, in other words, how well the candidate is expected to perform in the job. The algorithms, or the models, thus make predictions based on the data collected in the hiring process, and those who fit the KSAOs best should be hired.

As such, the process of digitalisation as it presents itself in hiring sees technologies deployed to collect data through, for instance, video interviews and games and in the assessment of the candidates through the development of models that predict from the data who based on the KSAOs is most likely to perform the job well. Therefore, candidate assessment not only moved from pen-and-paper to digital means but the way in which candidate fit is predicted changed with digitalisation. In addition, those people involved in the process change. Whereas before, human resource professionals in combination with industrial/organisational psychologists and the hiring managers would be involved in selection, the digitalised process of hiring also requires data scientists, AI specialists and programmers to be part of the hiring team. Often, specialist providers are employed by the recruiting company to handle different aspects of the digitalised recruitment process. For instance, one provider might specialise in CV screening, whereas another might provide assessment for online games, while yet others specialise in the assessment of recorded online interviews. This requires significant coordination work from all stakeholders to create digital selection procedures, but possibly the biggest change to the stakeholders involves the inclusion of data scientists, AI specialists and programmers in the hiring process.

Algorithmic Bias in Hiring

The best-known example of how AI-supported hiring can lead to replicating an existing pattern in regard to which candidates are seen as ideal certainly comes from Amazon. Amazon is well-known for its automation efforts, from pricing to warehouse management, and as such, it is perhaps not surprising that Amazon also tried to automate the process of selecting the best talent for the organisation (Dastin, 2018). Amazon thus designed an AI-driven tool that evaluated candidates' CVs and ranked them on suitability for engineering roles. The data that had been given to the AI tool to learn what the ideal candidate looks like was ten years' worth of CVs from existing employees in these functions. Most of those CVs belonged to men. As a consequence, everyone who had gone to a women's college or who was the 'women's chess club captain' was filtered out (Dastin, 2018). The AI tool learned that those who fit the template did not have anything with women on their CVs. This failed experiment of automating recruitment was widely discussed in the media and is endlessly recited as an example for algorithmic bias. We do not know in how far processes such as a job analysis to identify KSAOs and the various forms of validity described before were followed that should in theory safeguard against such unfairness. However, it functions as an example of the urgent need that if recruitment is automated, this requires input from specialists like industrial/organisational psychologists, diversity and inclusion specialists, and related disciplines.

This raises the question of how algorithmic bias can be defined. The technical understanding of algorithmic bias centres on errors: algorithmic bias occurs when an AI system produces an error, which leads to inequitable outcomes for different groups (Russell & Norvig, 2021). If the system has an error, the assumption is that this error can be fixed. An alternative understanding informed by science and technology studies (MacKenzie & Wajcman, 1999) offers a different approach to algorithmic bias. If technology is seen as a reflection of society and in society, bias is prevalent, technology that is produced by biased societies is also likely to exhibit this bias. Algorithmic bias is therefore not a 'bug' or error in the system but a central principle of how society works that has left traces in the technologies produced. By the same token, if there is a societal desire to create equality or equitable outcomes, technologies can be shaped to ensure that this is achieved. To recur to the technical language, algorithmic bias is fixable if technology is shaped accordingly.

Algorithmic bias is often linked to the underlying data used in digital technologies and particularly machine learning. For machine learning, a system is fed with training data based on which the system develops a model; in other words, it learns (Russell & Norvig, 2021). This model is then fine-tuned and applied to real-life data (Russell & Norvig, 2021). The training data used is therefore central for machine learning. In the Amazon example discussed earlier, the training data – ten years of CVs from existing employees – exhibited historical bias. Because the majority of people in the role were men, anything associated with women was seen as less suitable for the role. One can also speculate that given the lack of non-white, non-straight and non-binary individuals, such data sets will also likely show racial, sexuality and gender identity bias (Benjamin, 2019; Tomasev et al., 2021). If most people in the data set never had a career break, everyone who has gaps in their CV might also be ranked lower by such a system. As such, it is possible to see how such an approach might bring up a range of issues in machine learning if those systems are not designed to take account of such differences.

Relatedly, data can also be unrepresentative of the wider population. Recorded video interviews provide an example as to why this matters in the hiring process. In fact, such technologies are regularly criticised in the media for creating outcomes that can be unfair. Journalists, for instance, read the same text in such a recorded video interview while changing physical appearance by wearing glasses or a headscarf and their screen backgrounds (Harlan & Schnuck, 2023), with the consequence that every time, the system produced slightly different feedback. Such criticism has led providers like HireVue to drop facial analysis in their assessment of candidates (Knight, 2021). Part of the problem might be the underlying data used. The Gender Shades project has shown that darker women's faces were misgendered to a much higher rate than any other group; for one of the AI systems tested, the error rate was 34.4% between darker-skinned women's faces and lighter-skinned men's faces (Buolamwini & Gebru, 2018;

Gender Shades, 2023). One explanation for this that the underlying data set did not contain enough darker-skinned women, which providers of such data sets have started addressing. Due to persistent criticism of using video and associated facial expressions, some providers like HireVue, mentioned earlier, have dropped analysing video and only focus on voice. However, focusing on voice has issues in itself. If the voice data, for example, does not provide sufficient variation in regard to accents, specific language patterns or even tone of voice (Tippins, 2015), the technology might not be able to understand individuals.

A third facet of data bias relates to how data is actually collected. In HR, it is, for example, uncommon to collect data on those who have not been selected in a recruitment process, leaving only those who were hired in the pool of individuals that provide data (Tambe et al., 2019). HR data can also rely on assessments that might be subjective (Tambe et al., 2019). Let's look at an example from a professional services firm where employees were ranked in their annual performance reviews from 'zero' to 'five', with five being the highest performance. However, what does a manager do if a woman is on maternity leave? It was part of the company policy to still provide performance evaluations, and many managers selected 'three' because the women were not technically at work (Kelan, 2023a). For high-performing women who are normally ranked 'five', this was often the first time in their career that this has happened. Once such a subjective assessment is transferred into an objective number, it might be used as part of a data set for machine learning to hire new employees. If we presume that the average of those women on maternity leave is around 30, depending on what data is included the AI system might learn that women around 30 perform at a 'three' level and should not be a priority to be hired. How data is collected and which subjective decisions impact the data collection is as such crucial in regard to algorithmic bias.

AI systems are black boxes, which can make it difficult to understand how a system arrives at a prediction (Pasquale, 2015). In other words, the process of machine learning itself might lead to biased outcomes because it is often not clear what predictions are based on. In regard to gender, this crystallises, for instance, in the question of how gender might be inferred by an AI system. In recent years, HR has started to introduce more than two genders in HR data to include individuals who are non-binary, or who use other gender identifications (Smith, 2021). HR largely asks individuals to self-select the gender identification that is most appropriate for them. However, when it comes to the hiring process, such information cannot be used in most global locations because it is illegal to consider demographic characteristics in hiring. As such, the candidates are unlikely to have their self-selected gender identity appear in the data sets. One could now presume that any selection would be equal because demographic characteristics are not considered. However, in machine learning, proxies for protected characteristics might be created or the AI system might infer forbidden information (Kearns & Roth, 2019). This can happen through 'redundant encoding' (Dwork et al., 2012), where information that is not required or provided is inferred from data. A CV might contain a statement that the candidate is active in an LGBTQ network but an organisation has not hired many individuals who are active in an LGBTQ network before, which means that the candidate might be ranked lower than others (Tomasev et al., 2021). While gender identity and sexual orientation are not directly entered into the AI system, the AI system infers not a specific identity as such but rather that people with such a background are uncommon and do not match the criteria that were given, leading to the lower ranking. If social media data is used in hiring (Black et al., 2015) and a prospective candidate liked content about Black people, an AI might infer that this person is Black. Class might also be inferred in the same way (Wachter, 2020). Machine learning might also lead to the learning that those named 'Mary' do less well than those named 'Mark' and should therefore not be hired (Lee et al. 2019), or that frequenting certain Japanese cartoon websites means one is a better programmer (Dalenberg, 2018). This not only matters after a candidate has applied for a job but can even affect who sees specific job adverts in the first place, where race rather than qualification can influence what type of adverts one sees (Datta et al., 2014; Imana et al., 2021; Sweeney, 2013).

The fact that machine learning is often likened to a black box where it is unclear how a prediction is arrived at leads to a specific paradox when using AI systems in hiring. Kearns and Roth (2019) explain that it is indeed possible to optimise AI systems to not only minimise errors but also to avoid violating the principle of fairness. However, this approach requires the use of protected characteristics in the model. For example, one can check how many Black women over 30 are in the sample and balance the results internally through a process called inverse weight propensity scores (Kelan, 2024).[1] Another suggestion is to create an algorithm that compares an underrepresented group, for instance, women in science, technology, engineering, and mathematics (STEM), with other women in the sample rather than the overall population (Dwork et al., 2012). It might be possible that under certain conditions such as affirmative action programmes, such an approach might be legitimate; in most hiring situations, using such protected characteristics would be illegal. This leads to a paradoxical situation: in order to create fairness and equality, protected characteristics need to be included in models, yet doing so would violate anti-discrimination rules that are designed to create fairness. This paradox is central in how those who design AI for hiring address algorithmic bias.

Techno-Optimism or Constructing Algorithmic Bias as Fixable

In the interviews that I conducted, most people could be described as techno-optimists. The perspective of techno-optimism has been discussed, debated and questioned in philosophy (Danaher, 2022; Königs, 2022). Techno-optimism has been defined as 'the stance that holds that technology (…) plays a key role in ensuring that the good does or will prevail over the bad' (Danaher, 2022, p. 54). However, Königs questions this definition by arguing that '[t]he more important question, from a social and political point of view, is whether technology can be expected to improve the human condition or not' (Königs, 2022, p. 63). Even this definition, one might argue, would still be rather abstract for a person designing an AI-supported hiring system. However, the idea that technology improves the operations of a business or that AI improves the effectiveness of hiring is something one would regularly hear from practitioners in the field. While there is merit in discussing the finer nuances of the philosophical debate, for the purpose of this book, techno-optimism is defined as the stance that technology, such as AI, improves a business function, such as hiring. In other words, using AI is seen as superior to not using it.

Techno-optimism is not a surprising stance that those who design AI-hiring solutions would take; as a matter of fact, it is somewhat predictable that they would do. However, what interests me is how individuals negotiate the stance of techno-optimism with algorithmic bias; the underlying idea of techno-optimism is that technology improves business and is, in the wider sense, a force for good. However, algorithmic bias is a way in which inequalities might potentially increase, and as such, if the reduction of inequalities is seen as of positive value, then techno-optimism would not be necessarily a stance one can uphold. As such, my interest was on how people negotiate being techno-optimists with algorithmic bias.

Humans as Making AI Biased

Interviewees would commonly reference the fact that algorithmic bias only exists because humans have biases and AI learns such biases from humans. Lucy suggests that algorithms themselves are not biased but that the data that algorithms are trained with is. For Lucy, algorithms are just ways to run numbers, and they reinforce bias because they have been fed biased data. Franklin stated that humans are biased and that AI is amplifying this. In other words, the bias is already there and AI just makes it visible. Anton describes algorithmic bias as a human problem. He justifies his view by stating that human bias becomes manifest in data sets and in the machine learning process, those biases are learned by a machine. Anton suggests that AI simply copies biases from humans. One might presume that such algorithmic bias thus dampens the optimism for AI, but Anton in his next discursive move suggests that AI provides the unique opportunity to make human biases visible in a systematic way, and often for the first time. He acknowledges that biases existed before but they were hidden and AI makes them visible, tangible and, most importantly for Anton, addressable. Thereby, the stance of techno-optimism is retained by arguing that algorithmic bias is beneficial in so far as it makes human bias visible through technology. Howard made a similar argument. Howard argues that machine learning picks up the patterns from human behaviour and amplifies them, but it can also put a spotlight on those biases. Howard suggests that companies can use AI and machine learning to show them where they have discriminated in the past by analysing historic data. As such, patterns of discrimination can be made visible, which by consequence would be good for organisations. The discursive moves that Howard and Anton display are strikingly similar in that negative connotations of algorithmic bias are turned into a benefit of using AI.

A variation of this stance is that humans are biased. Henry talked about how humans are biased and therefore produce biased data. He states that recruiters and hiring managers often believe that they are excellent at hiring, but Henry is of the opinion that once you look at their rating, it becomes obvious that they are not very good at rating people, and by extension, identifying the most suitable person for the job. Henry, for instance, maintains that machines are less biased than human evaluators by giving the example of a study that looks at how hiring managers evaluate competence in female- and male-dominated occupations (he cites nurses and construction workers). He uses this study to suggest that the machine score was less biased than the human score. He concludes that if an algorithm is correctly designed, it is less biased than untrained human evaluators. Henry displays techno-optimism in so far as a well-designed and tested algorithm is constructed as superior to humans, not only in selecting the best-suited person but also in avoiding bias.

Humans generally appear as the bearers of bias in the decision-making process. Jasmine said, for instance, that AI-supported hiring is often used to make processes easier, but for her, the real benefit is that it standardises processes. Standardising processes increases fairness up until the point when human decision-makers have a say. This can happen, according to Jasmine, for example, in face-to-face interviews or when a human decision-maker is given the scores of the individuals that best fit the job but then only picks the men to take them further. For Jasmine, AI can be used to make hiring fairer and to reduce discrimination, but she suggests that once humans influence the decision-making process bias creeps back in. Like with Henry, Jasmine constructs AI as fairer than humans. She says that regardless of how much one tries to reduce bias in AI, because once human decision-makers enter the picture, bias can re-emerge. Such an idea is indeed supported by research, which has shown that using AI in recruitment can lead to a reduction in diversity, but that this is not due to algorithmic bias but rather due to the recruitment manager: the recruitment managers, for instance, might not follow the machine-generated ranking and thereby introduce bias (Bursell & Roumbanis, 2024).

Fixing the Data and the Rater

In order to maintain the stance of techno-optimism, it was common to argue that algorithmic bias is fixable. The discourse to suggest that algorithmic bias is fixable first of all related to data. This is not surprising because most people see data as the root cause of algorithmic bias, as we have seen earlier in this chapter. Ginny talked about that checking the training data that models learn from is paramount to avoid that the data is replicating biases. Kenneth suggested that training data needs to be diversified to create representative data sets, and he opines that big companies are already doing this. He further specifies how this is done: if you have a training data set based on 99% data from men and 1% data from women then it is necessary to balance the data input to 50% women and 50% men and to proceed accordingly in regard to race by including data based on 25% Black populations. Anton describes it as merely a 'technical problem' to build data sets that do not suffer from bias.

Isabel uses a similar argument but is more sceptical that changing the input will be enough. She maintains that if there are few data points for women and even fewer for Black women, then any predictions that an AI system reaches will be weaker for these groups. For her, the problem lies in historic data, which will always replicate the same outcomes. Instead, she suggests that completely new data sets need to be created, which is similar to what Kenneth mentioned. However, her approach to fix the data is different: in the hiring technology company where she works, they have decided not to use historic data at all. They do not use CVs and they do not use what 'good' looked like in the past. Instead, they are trying to build new data sets that do not suffer from historic bias. However, much of what she discusses relates to future developments where she is optimistic that one day, hiring decisions can be made without bias. This strong belief in the potential of technology and that algorithmic bias is fixable is a typical discursive move to maintain the perspective of techno-optimisms, in spite of the challenges associated with algorithmic bias.

Apart from fixing representation in data, fixing the human who produces input data was also flagged as important by many people I spoke with. While the fixing the data idea discussed before largely centred on changing representations, these arguments focused more on how data emerges. The classic example is that a manager might display gender bias and thus rate women lower in performance evaluations, which are then fed into HR systems (Edwards & Edwards, 2019). In some cases, the manager does not even have to be biased, but gendered data input can result from input that is well-intended but has the opposite effect. We might here think about the women that were ranked three out of five while on maternity leave, as mentioned earlier in this chapter. Although none of the interviewees used this specific example, human raters were mentioned in regard to how recorded interviews were scored. Such recorded interviews are often used in hiring, where on a hiring platform, a candidate is recording answers to specific questions via video. In this interaction, the interaction partner is actually the machine that poses questions and the interviewee answers. A common assumption is that those interviews are scored by AI. However, Kirsty and Ginny clarified that this is not the case. In Kirsty's organisations, such recorded interviews are scored by humans who are trained assessors who assess based on a matrix or rubric. The same is true for Ginny, who states that only 20% of recorded interviews are scored by machines, which means that 80% are scored by humans. Again, the humans are trained industrial/organisational psychologists who evaluate based on rubrics. These rubrics are developed by the industrial/organisational psychology team after conducting a job analysis to ensure that the correct competencies are measured. These competencies themselves are assessed through models that predict those competencies, and those models were developed in the company based on trained expert raters.

Ginny goes on to provide an example of how this works when a candidate is assessed in relation to customer service. In the recorded interview, candidates are asked to describe a time when they had to deal with a difficult customer. The organisation has thousands of examples of how other people answered this question, based on which the model, and the rubrics were developed and defined. The trained evaluators then evaluate the candidates' answers as good, medium or low, for example. Ginny describes how they originally thought that humans are biased and that therefore, the scoring would be biased too. However, they discovered that with this standardisation through rubrics and trained assessors, human bias is reduced. Ginny's argument suggests that the human bias in creating data can be minimised through training humans and assessing in rubrics. It fixes the messy and unruly human part, which Ginny describes as people going on their gut feeling based on unstructured interviews to make hiring decisions. This gut feeling Ginny suggests has impacted the hiring process in the past. If a gut feeling is used to hire candidates and this data is used in machine learning, the resulting hiring process will be saturated with human biases. By reducing this gut feeling and the human biases, the potential algorithmic bias in hiring is also reduced.

Henry also talked about improving algorithms. Henry who works in a hiring technology company insisted that 90% of his company's algorithms are based on human raters. In order to illustrate why this is important, he cited the saying that 'an algorithm is only as good as the data it's being modelled upon', which in machine learning is often described as 'garbage in, garbage out' (Weyerer & Langer, 2019). Henry explains that this means that if you have bias in the data, you are modelling bias in your algorithm. As such, it is central to avoid this bias in data input. To build their models, the company has multiple trained human evaluators evaluating each interview. They then check the agreement between the model and a human evaluator. As such, the predictive power of the models is measured against expert human predictions. Henry argues that by reducing the bias in human-rated data, the predictive models of AI can be improved. Like in Ginny's example, the idea that human variation in assessment makes algorithms biased, or more broadly that societal bias is shaping algorithmic bias, is being employed to advance the stance that human bias has to be reduced in data input to avoid algorithmic bias. This means that if human raters are 'fixed', algorithmic bias can be fixed too.

Fixing the Algorithm

Apart from fixing the data and the (human) rater, interviewees also suggested to fix the algorithm. This can take different forms. Franklin talked about a provider that removed any personal information from applications to ensure that candidates are evaluated based on skills. Among the information that is excluded is where the candidate worked before. Franklin suggests that big technology companies are dominated by men and the provider is removing this information to allow hiring managers to focus on skills rather than impressive sounding company names. The candidates' names, gender and race/ethnicity are also removed. Although it could be argued that removing such information from candidates' profiles reduces the ability of the AI to learn any bias and to influence the hiring manager, in most cases, much of such information would be revealed at later interview stages, at which point it can still influence hiring managers. Bradley similarly talked about ways in which algorithms are blinded by, for example, excluding if a candidate identifies as female or male, which are the two gender options Bradley mentions. According to Bradley, the idea is that algorithms then cannot distinguish between who is female and who is male and as such, bias might be reduced. Bradley is sceptical that such an approach ultimately works but he is aware that it exists.

Another approach of dealing with algorithmic bias through blinding the algorithm is provided by Henry. Henry talks about how his company has collected millions of recorded video interviews and they were able to detect gender and racial differences in how questions are answered and which words are used. He explains that men would use different words to women to describe certain competences. His company's approach is to 'blacklist' those words to avoid that they are included in the algorithm. Thereby, Henry suggests that the algorithm would not be influenced by gender differences in regard to which words are used to express competencies. Ginny suggests that the 'beauty of algorithms' is that even if the training data is biased, this can be mitigated in algorithms to avoid that this bias is reproduced. She acknowledges that you need to know what you are doing to avoid that. However, in her view, it is possible to control the algorithmic much more than the human mind. Ginny also suggests that information might be inferred by speech: women might talk more about childcare, whereas men talk about rugby. Her solution, similar to what Henry suggested, is to 'block' the words 'rugby' and 'childcare' to blind the algorithm for such gender differences. Such approaches suggest that it is possible to blind algorithm by either not including certain information or by blocking certain words. The idea is that if those inputs are not included in the predictions the algorithm makes, it is possible to control bias. Again, we see that the argument that it is easier to control algorithm than it is to control human minds is made, contributing to the view that if the algorithm is tamed by excluding human bias, it is possible to use algorithms to make recruitment fairer.

It was also common to talk about quality controls that are implemented in regard to algorithms. Lucy explained that in her company, a second algorithm was developed that checks the first algorithm for fairness. She expresses that this gives people confidence that the algorithm is not built on bias. Similarly, Kirsty acknowledges that no algorithm is perfect, like no selection tool is perfect. She, therefore, says that in her company, the algorithm is checked for adverse impact for different profiles every year, which allows 'tweaking' the algorithms if need be. Adverse impact is used in the United States to refer to 'the negative effect an unfair and biased selection procedure has on a protected class' (Mondragon, 2018), which can include, in the United States, sex, race, age and disability, among others. Duncan expresses a similar sentiment in regard to the fact that any algorithm that makes important decisions, such as who gets a job, should undergo quality assurance to ensure that there is clarity of what the algorithm measures.

Kenneth also suggests that one should engage an AI auditing company to assess the algorithms that are used, which is something that was done by many of the providers I spoke to. Kenneth, in particular, talks about A/B testing as important when auditing an algorithm. A/B testing is a randomised experiment that involves an A version and a B version to see if they perform differently. Kenneth gives the following example of what would happen if one looks for a top programmer. He suggests feeding the AI system with information from Black candidates and few white candidates and then comparing that to a different composition of candidates to see if there are differences in the result. If the AI system picks one of the few white men, he argues, and ignores the Black candidates, there might be bias in the algorithm.

Henry describes that once a model is built, his organisation follows up with an adverse impact analysis, which is what Kirsty mentioned earlier. This includes, as he says, to run statistics to see how men score versus women and evaluate the mean differences, the standard deviation differences and so on. Ideally, men and women should score as equally as possible and if there is a difference, one has to ask why that is and go back in to find why women and men score differently. Ginny provides further detail by arguing that there might be reasons why groups score differently, which would be fine from a legal perspective in the United States. This can include lifting heavy loads as a job requirement, which then would mean that more men than women might qualify. She describes this as a bona fide requirement. Ginny also talks about the four-fifth rule that is often used in regard to adverse impact in the United States. The four-fifth rule is a way to assess adverse impact through finding that the selection rate of one group is less than 80% of the group with the highest selection rate, as outlined in the Uniform Guidelines On Employee Selection Procedures (Biddle Consulting Group, 2023). However, Ginny asserts that while the four-fifth rule is often cited, one could clear this hurdle but might still find that there is unfairness. Ginny particularly points to subgroups that could be evaluated unfairly, such as top-performing women being evaluated differently than lower-performing women. As such, it is necessary to divide groups further to check in a more granular way that bias does not affect the model by including, for instance, information on performance. Although the four-fifth rule is regularly mentioned, Ginny, as well as others such as Alisha, stress that the four-fifth rule is not the *sine qua non* to assess equality and further tests are required to establish fairness.

Overall, it was often argued that a detailed assessment is required to ensure that algorithms do not produce bias. Most interviewees agreed that this is not an easy feat but that it could be used to ensure that algorithms are not producing biased predictions. In that way, the view that algorithms can be fixed supports the stance that machines can be de-biased. This in turn supports a techno-optimist's perspective.

Machines Do Not Make Hiring Decisions, Humans Do

However, there was also a stance that cautioned against the use of AI in hiring. Those perspectives were not techno-pessimistic in the sense that technology was seen as leading to poorer outcomes. This stance was characterised by being hesitant to use AI in hiring. This stance was not an outright rejection of AI in general but a hesitation of using AI at this point in time.

Most of the interviewees suggested that algorithms could be fixed, but Alisha goes further in agreeing that sometimes an algorithmic fix can be found, for instance, in a hiring algorithm where it is possible to fix the data or the model. Yet, this was for Alisha just a stopgap measure until one is able to find a better solution. She specifies that by better, in this context, she means more equitable. However, for her, technologies are often used to ignore problems around inequalities. She goes on to explain that people often hide behind the veneer of the algorithm. Alisha specifically states that algorithms are said to be based on data and that implies that hiring becomes more objective if algorithms are used. This in fact chimes with a perspective that I outlined earlier in this chapter in regard to techno-optimism. However, Alisha argues that sometimes algorithms are simply tools to 'ignore difficult conversations'. She suggests that these are difficult conversations about inequalities. As such, she concludes that people simply hide behind algorithms and their presumed objectiveness without addressing inequalities in a more profound way.

However, Alisha was the only person mobilising the idea that algorithms are a veneer or something to hide behind. It was far more common to suggest that algorithms improve human decision-making. Lucy stressed that algorithms should not make all decisions but instead, they make recommendations that can then be taken further with human knowledge. As such, she points to the importance that humans are in the driver's seat when it comes to making decisions. Lucy qualifies her statement by saying that humans obviously need to understand how the algorithm arrives at a suggestion. In a similar vein, Jasmine supports the idea that AI-supported hiring is fairer but she also says that human oversight over decisions is important. Henry was more specific in that he suggested that a machine allows people to make better decisions. He agreed that a machine should not make the actual decision but a machine can assist humans in improving decisions. Henry justifies this point of view by saying that the machine will use standardised and consistent data, which in turn can help humans to be less biased. As such, these ideas of how machines and humans collaborate still follow the idea of techno-optimism in so far as they are used to suggest that human decision-making will improve, leading to better decision.

Again, Alisha was slightly more hesitant about this machine–human collaboration. Alisha contests the idea that hiring managers are all powerful. She agrees that they have some power in organisations but she points out that the AI system has to be designed in such a way that allows the hiring manager to question the algorithm or to even overturn the recommendation. As such, she insists that humans would be able to contradict the predictions a machine makes. However, Alisha is not sure if humans will actually do that. For instance, if a candidate is suggested by a machine, would a human question this judgement or would the human pick the path of least resistance and follow what the machine recommended. For Alisha, that is a question of human nature, where picking the path of least resistance is common. Furthermore, she acknowledges that systems often do not allow for dissent. A hiring manager might have less opportunities to question the prediction of an ideal candidate of a machine because the system has not been built with this in mind.

When I spoke with Franklin about the risks of using only candidates that a machine has suggested, Franklin recalls a conversation with one of his clients who historically has recruited the top people by going with who is on top of the stack. However, this client said that people further down the list are often less in demand and they show great developmental potential. Franklin suggests that candidates in the middle of the pile would ultimately be better people to hire in the long run. This risk of only hiring the best-suited person for the job rather hiring mid-range people who might be able to develop is however not a function of using AI in hiring. As a matter of fact, much of how recruitment is done is focusing on the person who best fits the specification one has set out. This is codified in the Uniform Guidelines On Employee Selection Procedures (Biddle Consulting Group, 2023), which, as I mentioned before, is regularly used when hiring. Algorithms mechanise this process and therefore intensify the focus on those who best fit the criteria set out.

Yet, it has been argued that there is a benefit in going for a 'wildcard' hire from time to time to break the patterns that have been established over time of what skills are required to do a job (Tambe et al., 2019). A more developmental perspective of hiring would depart from much of how hiring looks like at this point in time. There is a risk that using machines to mechanise hiring leads to an even narrower focus on those who match the skills required best. While much concern is currently on eradicating bias from AI hiring processes by, for example, blocking language that might give away gender or race, there is a wider question in how far skills that are assessed might disadvantage those who have not developed those skills yet but who could do so in the future. At the moment, skills that are assessed in hiring are more baseline skills and often not something that cannot be changed much. For instance, the 'Big Five' personality assessment, on which much hiring is based, assesses extraversion or if one is outgoing. If it has been established that a salesperson should be outgoing and thus high on extraversion, this fits the current model of a salesperson. One could presume that the use of technology is leading to this profile of the salesperson as extravert is getting more and more refined. However, for machine learning, breaking those patterns with a 'wildcard' might be as useful. As such, standardising recruitment might be beneficial to reduce bias in the hiring process, but picking someone unusual might be helpful to introduce variations in patterns.

However, such wider reflections, which could be described as techno-hesitation, were rarely brought up in the interviews. While some people reflected on how humans and machines collaborate in decision-making, it was also clear that it is not the case that an AI makes a hiring decision without human influence. AI filters people out that do not fit the skills profile identified but AI will not make the final hiring decision. As such, AI is largely used to create a shortlist to identify people who can then be evaluated by humans. Kirsty describes hiring in her organisation as a 'mass rejection system'. Since the organisation receives a lot more applications than it has positions, AI in hiring is used to reject those people that do not fit the skills profile. However, the more advanced the hiring process gets, the more involved human decision-makers are in the process. As such, the techno-hesitation is in this case mainly an expression of the fact that AI will not make hiring decisions but is rather rejecting individuals that do not fit well. However, such wider issues about if humans can contradict the prediction of an algorithm or if hiring the best-suited candidate is always the best strategy were only raised on the margins of the discussions.

Reputational Risks

Techno-hesitation was also expressed through a concern for reputational risk. This included not trusting the idea that AI will always be the best solution for a problem. The idea that technology is always the solution to a problem is called techno-chauvinism (Broussard, 2018). Alisha invokes techno-chauvinism when stating that technology is always the solution. Similarly, Franklin discussed how he was approached by a senior leader in a Fortune 100 company who, as Franklin asserts, was in a bit of a panic because the company had realised that one of their competitors was using AI in hiring. The leader came to Franklin saying that he needed some AI to use in the hiring process to keep up with the competition. Franklin advised that it first needs to be clarified what problem AI is supposed to solve in regard to HR and to be open to the possibility that AI might not be the solution to the problem. Franklin suggested that chasing the competition without trying to solve a specific problem should not be enough of a reason to use AI, but one can imagine that such a bandwagoning is one reason why many organisations look into AI for hiring and beyond.

Another central concern in regard to AI in hiring is related to negative publicity that organisations might receive for using AI in hiring. Esme talked about one of her clients where the client did not do due diligence, went with the shiny promise of an AI provider and only discovered later that the science behind the AI was sketchy. Esme talks about how some providers in the field of AI hiring promise a lot but do not have the right basis in place to uphold such promises. This is why using AI in hiring is often likened to snake oil. Esme also talked about intelligent sourcing; intelligent sourcing, she explains, is that one uses the data from a CV to then harvest data in social media on this person to provide some insight on the candidate. She also mentioned a different provider who offers 90-second assessments through a visual personality questionnaire. Esme acknowledges that this is used in the United States but her company has been unable to sell it to clients in the UK because her clients in the UK did not trust that such assessments could be made in 90 seconds. AI in hiring is not generally seen as negative in the interviews but there is some hesitation that the underlying science is sound.

Other organisations conduct internal checks as part of their due diligence. Kirsty recounts that in her organisation, the AI capability team checked an AI of a potential provider for a hiring solution and found that the model lacked explainability. Kirsty expands on this by saying that the AI capability team was not convinced that there is no bias. Kirsty's company subsequently decided not to use the AI hiring provider because they were not comfortable with it. She constructs this is a good decision and points to media reporting about similar issues that other companies experienced when trying to use AI in hiring. Kirsty said that reputational concerns were paramount when her company decided against using this technology. Kirsty acknowledges that the market might shift eventually but at the moment, her organisation's key priority is to protect the brand. By 'a shift in the market', Kirsty means that AI in hiring is widely accepted and that negative reporting in the press is reduced. Kirsty describes negative press reporting as 'negative spin' and 'negative publicity'. As such, the reason for not using AI are not the biases as such but rather than reputational risks if the company is using AI in hiring and the media reports negatively on that.

Apart from reputational risks associated with negative media reports, many interviewees also talked about the legal risks associated with AI in hiring. Esme said that many of her clients are hesitant to adopt AI in hiring because they are concerned about lawsuits, especially in the United States. Many of those concerns were expressed in regard to feedback that candidates receive. Ginny describes the United States as a litigious society and states that many companies in the United States do not like providing candidate feedback because they are afraid that they will be sued. Jasmine voiced a similar concern in regard to the United States but mentioned that this is different in the EU. Henry elaborated on a similar point by saying that in the EU, the General Data Protection Regulation requires that feedback is provided to candidates, whereas in the United States, companies are fearful of giving feedback to candidates because candidates could take legal action. As such, Anton argues that many clients find it easier not to share 'too much' with candidates to avoid being involved in any lawsuits.

Techno-hesitation should thus be considered within the context in which AI is being deployed at the moment. Techno-hesitation relates to whether a human or a machine is making the hiring decision and the potential for reputational damage that goes with negative press reporting or being sued. However, this context might change if either the media is no longer interested in reporting on when AI-supported hiring goes wrong or when legal rights for candidates are being clarified further. There was not a concern that AI was indeed biased and could not be fixed like a techno-pessimistic stance might entail. Instead, the idea that lies behind such statements is there are some providers who 'oversell' the predictive power of their models combined with the fact that society is in many cases constructed as not ready for AI. There was the expectation that this will change over time, with providers being more rigorous in regard to their models, the media being less interested in exposing employers, and the legal system adapting to the use of AI in hiring. The tenor thus was that society might not be ready just yet to accept AI in hiring but that can change over time. Therefore, there was some hesitation to use AI for hiring at this point in time but this techno-hesitation might wither away as AI in hiring becomes more accepted.

Conclusion

Hiring is in many ways about patterns – finding out which type of person an organisation needs for a position and then applying this pattern when recruiting new individuals to the organisation. Yet, these patterns have historically been shown to exclude those who are different from the norm. The common argument suggests that those in hiring decisions were biased towards a certain type of person, which meant that others were excluded. AI now promises to eradicate this human bias by standardising the recruitment process. This contributes to what I have called a techno-optimist's dream of hiring using AI in hiring. In this dream, a machine spouts out the person that is best suited to perform well in the vacant position. In reality, machines are currently largely used to filter out candidates that do not match the required profile well enough to present hiring managers with a selection of candidates that best fulfil the requirements. It is also evident that it is humans who make the hiring decision and human input is required at almost all stages of the hiring process. There is nevertheless a concern that if the machines that screen the candidates are biased, this will contribute to replicating if not amplifying inequalities.

The chapter centred on exploring how the techno-optimist stance that technology improves processes such as hiring can be reconciled with the problem that algorithmic bias can contribute to inequalities. Most interviewees were supporting a techno-optimist's stance in so far as they supported the idea that AI in hiring is generally an improvement over hiring without AI. Much of the argument centred on the idea that algorithmic bias, while problematic, is ultimately fixable through a set of interventions. AI was constructed as biased because humans are biased and AI is learning from and thus copying human biases. In order to fix bias, it was suggested to follow three strategies: first, fix the data; second, to fix the human raters who produce the data; and third, to fix the algorithm. The stance of techno-optimism was supplemented by the stance of what I called techno-hesitation. Techno-hesitation as a stance meant that people insisted that humans rather than machines make the final hiring decisions. It also entails concern about negative media coverage and lawsuits. However, this was not a techno-pessimism where technology in general was seen as leading to problematic organisational processes but a wait-and-see stance, which acknowledged that AI-supported hiring will become normalised over time.

The chapter has thus shown how the potential for AI in hiring was constructed as a way to eradicate human bias in a systematic and scalable way through technology. In order to maintain a techno-optimist's stance, algorithmic bias was thus constructed as ultimately fixable. However, such a perspective neglects that AI picks up many social patterns and replicates them. Fixing algorithmic bias is the attempt to change these patterns. However, without a thorough understanding of how technologies are shaped by society and vice versa, changing these patterns will be a futile exercise. The chapter has also suggested that technology is used to make hiring processes objective. In Chapter 5, I will explore how this presumed objectivity of technology is achieved.

Note

1 Thanks to Dr. Ana Matran-Fernandez for this suggestion.

5

IN/VISIBILITY BY DESIGN

Introduction

How does a machine know if a person is a woman, a man or non-binary? One option, and possibly the most straightforward one, is that a person indicates their preferred gender during data input. People then have the option to select or define how they identify. Another option is that during machine learning, the AI system might infer from data that the person is a woman. For example, in Chapter 4, Ginny showed how a machine might deduct from words who is a man or a woman. There are many proxies for gender in data through which gender can be inferred. Finally, a person who engages in data labelling work could be entering gender with an annotation. For example, if one has to label a picture, one might select the label 'woman' when annotating the data. As we have seen in Chapter 4, if one aims to reduce algorithmic bias, gender labels for data are important, which are often added by data labellers or data annotators.[1] It is thus important to explore such data practices to ascertain how they hinder or foster inclusion.

This chapter explores how data labels construct a world that is knowable for machine learning systems. In order to make predictions about the world, a machine learning system needs to understand what is depicted in

DOI: 10.4324/9781003427100-5

a picture or what words are linked to specific sounds. This happens through labels that connect an image or sound with a word that the computer can understand. Designers of AI commonly develop classifications of labels that then need to be connected to data. These labels are often assigned to data by workers in the Global South either as crowd work or in more traditional employment forms. While the working conditions of these workers are regularly the focus of attention, these workers also play a central role in creating data sets that are constructed as universal and objective, even though they are based on complex processes of meaning making entailed in such assessments. The chapter shows how these subjective processes of knowing are harmonised and standardised as an objective truth in data labelling. It is also discussed that many of the classifications used are exclusionary. For instance, gender labels are commonly conceived as a binary. This chapter thus traces how data labelling constructs a knowable world. The chapter focuses on the mechanisms of construction and the international division of labour that these processes entail.

AI's Hidden Workforce

If people picture someone who works in AI, the images that are conjured up include highly paid data scientists, probably white, a man and based in Silicon Valley. However, much of the work that allows AI to learn is done by data annotators who label data, which in turn allows for machine learning to happen. When ChatGPT, a chatbot developed by OpenAI, was publicly launched in November 2022, many people marvelled at ChatGPT's ability to generate text that is hard to distinguish from what a human might write (Mollick, 2022; Abdullah et al., 2022). However, unlike previous chatbots such as Microsoft's Tay (Vincent, 2016), ChatGPT did not produce racist and sexist talk. That is not a coincidence. The previous version of the technology had in fact a tendency to produce racist and sexist talk (Perrigo, 2023). In order to avoid that, OpenAI ensured that anything that could be seen as racist and sexist would be filtered out in ChatGPT's answers (Perrigo, 2023). However, to determine what is racist and sexist, the AI system needed to learn what racism and sexism look like. The data for ChatGPT was scraped from the internet. This inevitably included data that could be seen as racist and sexist. Since OpenAI wanted to avoid that ChatGPT reproduces racist and sexist language, the system had to learn what such language looks like.

In order to identify racist and sexist language, OpenAI followed a similar approach that is used by, for instance, Meta's Facebook to filter out toxic language. This approach requires humans to label any data that is sexist and racist to ensure that it can be excluded from the AI output that a chatbot like ChatGPT might produce (Perrigo, 2023). This required human data annotators to label data that could be seen as racist or sexist (Perrigo, 2023). Such human-in-the-loop approaches are often outsourced to organisations in the Global South. This human input is often invisible and left out of focus when the presumed achievements of AI are marvelled at.

Hiding the human input in technology is in fact not a new phenomenon. Amazon's MTurk is a case in point. MTurk stands for Mechanical Turk and is thus a reference to a 18th-century life-size chess-playing automaton that was dressed in Ottoman clothing (Stephens, 2023; Geoghegan, 2020; Gray & Suri, 2019; Standage, 2002) (see also Chapter 1). Wolfgang von Kempelen developed the automaton and presented it for the first time in 1770 at the Habsburg court, and it then was exhibited in Europe and the United States (Stephens, 2023; Geoghegan, 2020). The chess-playing automaton pretended to be a machine that played and often won against humans. However, instead of being an automated chess machine, the automaton required a human hiding in the machine who performed the chess moves that were then translated via mechanics to the chess board (Irani, 2015; Stephens, 2023; Geoghegan, 2020; Standage, 2002). As many people at the time already presumed, the Turk turned out to be a hoax (Stephens, 2023). However, as Standage suggests, the arrival of the automaton

> coincided with the beginnings of the industrial revolution, when machines first began to displace human workers, and the relationship between people and machines was being redefined. The chess player posed a challenge to anyone who took refuge in the idea that machine might be able to outperform humans physically but could not outdo them mentally.
>
> (Standage, 2002, p. xiv)

It was particularly the automaton's presumed ability to interact with its opponents during the chess game that was deemed implausible because it required machine intelligence (Standage, 2002). Not surprisingly, the activity of playing chess is still seen as one way of evaluating machine intelligence against that of humans (Standage, 2002). The Mechanical Turk thus raised the spectre that machines can replace human intelligence and not just the physical power of humans (Standage, 2002). As we have seen in Chapter 3, a similar question is raised today in regard to what skills are uniquely human and if machines are able to emulate emotions, which up to now have been seen as a human advantage.

But why was the automaton called the Turk? Although von Kempelen never named the automaton a Turk, the automaton wore Ottoman dress, which led to the name Turk. The reason why the automaton was dressed in Ottoman dress expresses a form of Orientalism but also reflects the long-standing rivalry between the Ottoman and the Habsburg empires including the Turkish siege of Vienna (Geoghegan, 2020). It has also been suggested that the Turkish style was popular in Vienna at the time (Standage, 2002). Another reason that the name Turk was adopted might in fact relate to German language, where the verb 'türken' translates as 'to turk' and means 'to fake'. The verb has strong pejorative connotations, which is why it is seen as discriminatory and should be avoided (Duden, 2023; Geoghegan, 2020). The etymology of the verb 'türken' is unclear (Duden, 2023; Geoghegan, 2020) and one potential origin of the verb in fact goes back to the Mechanical Turk being a fake (Geoghegan, 2020). Yet, neither the origins of the verb nor the origins of the automaton have been conclusively shown.

The name MTurk, which Amazon has chosen for its services, is reminiscent of von Kempelen's automaton. The MTurk service developed out of Amazon's attempts to reduce the number of duplicate listings (Stephens, 2023; Irani, 2015). Amazon tried to automate this action but failed because '[t]he task required a certain type of pattern recognition – the ability to detect subtle differences and similarities between pictures and text – which were easy for a human brain but could not be replicated by computer (sic)' (Stephens, 2023, p. 66). In other words, there are certain patterns that only humans can recognise. Therefore, Amazon decided to give small, individual tasks to workers who could complete the tasks in piecemeal work (Stephens, 2023). Amazon then offered the service to other clients, leading to the development of the platform MTurk, where clients', or requesters', tasks were matched with people willing to do these micro tasks for often small amounts of money (Stephens, 2023). As mentioned before, such approaches are often called 'human-in-the-loop'. A human-in-the-loop approach is required when human intelligence is needed to complete a task. Jeff Bezos calls MTurk 'artificial artificial intelligence' (Stephens, 2023).[2]

MTurk became emblematic for crowdsourced platform work (Irani, 2015; Howcroft & Bergvall-Kåreborn, 2019). As Howcroft and Bergvall-Kåreborn state, '[o]nline task crowdwork offers paid work (sometimes subject to requester satisfaction) for specified tasks and the initiating actor is the requester' (Howcroft & Bergvall-Kåreborn, 2019, p. 26). Research on MTurk and other platforms has regularly stressed the exploitative nature of these types of work (Irani, 2015; Howcroft & Bergvall-Kåreborn, 2019). Apart from being often seen as economically precarious work, the work can also leave individuals mentally scarred; it has been argued that mental health issues arise in many people who moderate social media content (Bui, 2020; Irani, 2016). In their ground-breaking study, Gray and Suri (2019) describe such work as 'ghost work' because we often presume that the work is done by a machine but in fact the work is completed by humans. An example is security background checks for Uber drivers where the driver has grown a beard and as such no longer matches the image on file; a human is then tasked to determine if the person signing in as a driver is indeed the same as the person on file (Gray & Suri, 2019). Through their detailed study of platform work, Gray and Suri (2019) show how 'algorithmic cruelty' is affecting individuals engaging in this work. They detail the struggle to find work and get paid, and the isolation entailed in these types of workplaces (Gray & Suri, 2019).

Due to the criticism of platform work as being exploitative, many companies have started to engage in practices of sustainable sourcing by outsourcing such work to providers that offer stable employment conditions for their workers (Gray & Suri, 2019). In attempts to make supply chains more sustainable, organisations that require moderation of social media data or data annotation have started to prefer suppliers like Sama or iMerit, whose mission is to offer work and thus a livelihood to individuals in the Global South (Perrigo, 2022,2023; Murgia, 2019). Although these workplaces have been lauded as the vanguard of AI (Murgia, 2019), it has also been reported that those workplaces can be exploitative in their own right (Perrigo, 2022, 2023; Pilling & Murgia, 2023, 2023, 2023; Pilling, 2024). As mentioned before, such work of moderating social media or labelling offensive language often leaves employees in such firms psychologically scarred (Perrigo, 2022; Pilling & Murgia, 2023; Pilling, 2024). It is suggested that for AI to work in the Global North, workers in the Global South have to put their mental health on the line[3] (Perrigo, 2022). As such, efforts to ensure that technologies are free from sexist, racist and harmful language and imagery are often met by the challenges of global supply chains.

The Need for Data Annotation

Although working conditions are rightly at the centre of many discussions on data annotation, at this point, it is useful to explore why data annotation or data labelling is needed in AI in the first instance. In a nutshell, machine learning, a subset of AI, is often described as a pattern recogniser – a pattern is spotted and this is used to make predictions (Caliskan et al., 2017). Not all machine learning requires labelled data. In unsupervised machine learning, data labels are not required, but for supervised machine learning, data needs to be labelled (Bechmann & Bowker, 2019). For supervised machine learning, some data might already be labelled in the data set, which are then used to build models. In other cases, the data might require labelling. For instance, for self-driving cars, it is necessary for a machine to be able to read how a stop sign looks, what a bus looks like or how humans of different shapes and sizes appear. Such image data thus has to be labelled to tell the machine exactly what a stop sign looks like. A similar process is followed for language that is, for instance, required for voice recognition software. As such, data annotators have to label images or language in data sets that can then be used for machine learning. Most of us engage in data labelling free of charge: when asked to prove that we are not a robot in online interactions, we have to, for example, select all pictures that have a motorcycle in it. The fact that we need to identify images and texts to show our humanity illustrates that machines struggle with this activity, creating the need for humans to label data in the first place.

Data has to be labelled to establish something that is called 'ground truth'. Ground truth is a term used in computer science and data science and is central for how data is used in algorithms (Jaton 2017, 2021). Jaton (2017, 2021) describes how ground truth is relevant in supervised machine learning: one starts with a data set and this data set is labelled by humans with clear targets (e.g. road signs, cars, humans), which the algorithm will have to identify. If there is disagreement among data labellers on how to label data, often, the majority vote is used to establish what should count as ground truth (McCluskey et al., 2021). The labelled data and the unlabelled data form a database that is called ground truth (Jaton, 2017). More specifically, 'ground truth refers to information that is assumed to be true for an (sic) ML [machine learning] system' (Kang, 2023, p. 1). The data set is then split into a training set and an evaluation set (Jaton, 2017, 2021). The training set allows the designers to 'extract formal information about the targets and translate them into mathematical expressions' (Jaton, 2017, p. 815). These mathematical expressions are then transformed into code and the algorithm is tested on the other set, which is called the evaluation set (Jaton, 2017, 2021). It is then assessed if the algorithm functioned as expected by comparing the result with the data labels assigned by humans (Jaton, 2017, 2021). The ground truth is thus based on the labels humans have assigned to data and allows to check for the correctness of the algorithm (Grosman & Reigeluth, 2019). The ground truth is as such a way to compare what a machine learned with what human labellers judged to be the case. The human labour that goes into developing an algorithm and seeing how well it is performing is central. In other words, the human labelling data helps machines to know what is true.

Although the name – ground truth – suggests objectivity, establishing ground truth is an interpretive practice (Miceli et al., 2020; Henriksen & Bechmann, 2020; Paullada et al., 2021). Data labellers commonly receive instructions on how to label a text or an image from the designers of AI, which has been described as a way in which power from the designers of AI onto the people who label data is exerted (Miceli et al., 2020). How the designers of AI establish those classifications has been described as subjective, and in some cases, arbitrary, and these classifications are then created and perpetuated through AI systems (Miceli et al., 2020; Noble, 2018; Eubanks, V., 2018). Within the confines of the descriptions provided by the designers of AI, the data labellers often have to make subjective decisions (Miceli et al., 2020). This means that data annotation is a sense-making practice (Miceli et al., 2020). Therefore, data labellers might disagree on how to label data. As previously mentioned, the majority vote is regularly used in such cases (McCluskey et al., 2021). However, using a majority vote obscures instances where data annotators systematically disagree which is particularly important in subjective tasks, like assessing hate speech or affect (Davani et al., 2022). If the disagreement is taken into consideration when models are being built, the resulting models are suggested to perform better (Davani et al., 2022). In consequence, taking the subjectivity of decisions that data annotators might make into consideration is important. However, in the process of machine learning, these subjective decisions are often obscured behind a presumed objectivity derived through majority votes. Even the name, ground truth implies depicting an objective reality. Yet, research has shown that presumed objective categories are regularly based on interpretation (Bowker & Star, 2000). Although the issue of data annotation and subjective decision-making is often raised in regard to supervised learning, it has been shown that unsupervised learning also relies on human supervision in regard to, for example, data cleaning or setting the number of topics (Bechmann & Bowker, 2019). Even the inclusion or exclusion of data in a data set can be seen as a way in which contextual factors influence and shape what the machine can learn (Denton et al., 2020; Miceli et al., 2020).

Since data set are pivotal for machine learning, it has been suggested that data sets should come with datasheets that describe why the data was collected, what the data is composed of, how the data was collected, and what the data should be used for, among other issues (Gebru et al., 2021). A similar approach is also followed in the electronics industry, where datasheets are created for each component that details test results, usage and operating characteristics (Gebru et al., 2021). Other similar approaches are followed for drugs, which are accompanied by information on how to use and what the side effects might be. Including datasheets for data sets could, for instance, entail information on which subpopulations are included and how they are distributed in the data set (Gebru et al., 2021). In regard to data collection, it should be considered which crowd workers were used and how they were compensated (Gebru et al., 2021). Similarly, in their sixth principle of data feminism, D'Ignazio and Klein (2020) discuss how context is relevant for data collection. They argue that data is not neutral and that the context in which the data is collected, analysed and communicated is important to make power dynamics visible (D'Ignazio & Klein, 2020). In an empirical application of those concepts, Miceli and co-authors (2021) ask how the context of production in data image sets can be made visible. They show that clients are generally responsible for defining classifications based on which, for example, race should be labelled in the data. Clients are in the driving seat in regard to defining these classifications and categories. Given the fact that clients are often based in the Global North, whereas the labellers are often based in the Global South, this also introduces a power dynamic (Miceli et al., 2021). The research also stresses that organisations might be hesitant to extensively document the context in which data sets are created due to the time, effort and complexity involved in doing so (Miceli et al., 2021). As such, it is vital to develop effective ways of including the context in which data sets are created, including the power dynamics at play in any datasheets for data sets provided.

Humans are centrally important for helping machines learn by recognising and labelling patterns. This process needs to be understood as a subjective one. As such, any subjective decisions, for example, associated with defining categories need to be recognised as such by documenting those decisions. Additionally, data sets need not only include information on how subjective decisions were made but also on the workers who label the data and as such introduce their own subjective decision-making in the process. Data sets need to include details on the context in which those decisions are being taken, such as the labour conditions of those who label data as well as the power dynamics between the client in the Global North and the provider often in the Global South. Thereby, it would be possible to make the human labour and the subjective decision-making that goes into data sets visible.

Classifying the World

Classification is a central activity for machine learning but the political dimension of classification is often ignored (Crawford, 2021). Bowker and Star (2000) describe the act of classifying or as they call it 'sorting things out' as deeply human. In other words, classifications are a form of organising the world. A classification is defined as a 'spatial, temporal or spatio-temporal segmentation of the world' (Bowker & Star, 2000, p. 10). Ideal classifications follow unique and consistent principles such as a temporal order (Bowker & Star, 2000). Categories are mutually exclusive and each instance fits into just one category (Bowker & Star, 2000). Ideally a classification system covers all potential instances, but this ideal is never fully achieved in reality (Bowker & Star, 2000). '[C]lassifications are powerful technologies' (Bowker & Star, 2000, p. 319), which by being embedded in infrastructures become invisible. This is central to how they unfold their power. As such, Bowker and Star (2000) argue for recognising the architectures of classifications as political and for challenging the taken for granted status that classifications often have. Crawford (2021) draws attention to the fact that AI is based on classifications that are embedded in infrastructure and that are political. However, training data sets and AI infrastructure are regularly seen as 'purely technical', even though 'they naturalize a particular ordering of the world which produces effects that are seen to justify their original ordering' (Crawford, 2021, p. 139).

In classifications around gender and race, the presumed ideal is that categories are clearly definable, clear cut and mutually exclusive. Gender and race are treated as automatically detectable and as something that can be predicted by AI systems (Crawford, 2021). It is common for data sets to follow a binary classification of gender such as using one for female and zero for male and an equally under complex classification for race of maybe five groups (Crawford, 2021). This is highly problematic as the example of how IBM tried to deal with algorithmic bias shows: IBM aimed to increase the diversity in data on facial recognition and they asked crowd workers to label faces as either male or female on a binary classification; yet anyone who was not neatly fitting into this binary was excluded from the data set (Crawford, 2021). When tracing how classifications are used in ImageNet, an image database, Crawford (2021) shows how available classifications under 'adult body' contain 'adult male body' and 'adult female body', where male and female are naturalised. Here, gender is classified in biological terms and as a binary. There is an option for 'hermaphrodite' but this is classified under bisexual (Crawford, 2021). Crawford (2021) concluded that non-binary individuals are either ignored or placed in a category related to sexuality. This means, as Crawford (2021, p. 146) suggests, '[m]achine learning systems are (…) *constructing* race and gender: they are defining the world within the terms they have set' (italics in original). Yet, these systems hide the politics entailed in their construction, which privileges clear-cut categories over the complexities of everyday life. These classifications are not only ordering the present but they are, through AI systems, also perpetuated in the future structuring of how the world is classified in the years to come.

Following the idea that machines are constructing gender, it is evident that for machine learning to happen, gender as a category has to be constructed. This entails to define what gender is and to operationalise gender to allow a machine to recognise gender (Keyes, 2018). How gender is defined and operationalised in machine learning has an effect on how gender is predicted (Keyes, 2018). This is happening, for instance, in Automatic Gender Recognition, where gender is 'read' from photographs (Keyes, 2018). The gender binary has long been questioned by research (Butler, 1990; Fausto-Sterling, 2000) but an analysis of papers on human–computer interaction has shown that gender is treated as a binary 94.8% of the time (Keyes, 2018). The research also found that gender is not only operationalised as binary but also as physiological and immutable (Keyes, 2018). Keyes (2018) suggests that this can be relevant, for instance, in regard to billboards that should show dresses to women and cars to men; if a transman passes such a billboard and is shown dresses, the billboard will have concluded that the transman is a woman. A consequence of this is that transgender individuals are likely to be misclassified, misgendered and ultimately erased (Keyes, 2018). It is therefore important to explore how AI produces a specific version of reality by exploring, for example, who is seen as a woman in facial recognition systems (Drage & Frabetti, 2023). As such, a machine is reading the gender of a person through a binary classification system that is then reproduced in the predictions made.

Helping AI to Understand the World

In order to illustrate how data practices help AI understand the world, I would now like to turn to how people I interviewed spoke about such practices. First, many interviewees addressed why data labelling is needed in the first place. Kenneth suggested that only about 30% of data labelling is automated today. Kenneth explained that AI is unable to recognise mountains in a picture or a middle-aged man. For machine learning to happen, a picture needs to be labelled with such information to be trained. Kenneth states that AI needs to have data that is labelled with information such as what is a cat and what is a dog, and for this, data labelling is important. Howard mentions how machines learn by example and can only do that if data is labelled, and like Kenneth, he references that an AI needs to know what a cat is and what a dog is. Similarly, Nicole used cats and dogs to explain why data has to be labelled: it has to be defined what dogs look like and what cats look like, and images have to be labelled as such to allow a computer vision system to make accurate predictions if an image contains a cat or a dog. Twyla also used the example of cats and dogs. It is not surprising that cats and dogs came up regularly in the interviews because it is a standard example used in machine learning. This is on the one hand due to the fact that cats and dogs are easily recognised by humans but not machines and on the other hand due to the fact that there is a lot of data on cats and dogs on the internet (Domingos, 2015; Mahardi et al., 2020).

Orlando used a slightly different example when explaining why data has to be labelled: he explains that children learn what an apple looks like through their parents and then apply a label. He likens this to how computers learn. Ralf, who works for a data annotation company, explains that AI needs to learn like a human needs to learn, but rather than sitting in classrooms, AI learns through training data. The computer needs data points to associate, as Ralf explains, a picture or a sound with a word, and the computer needs millions of those examples to be able to predict what computers are seeing or hearing. As such, Ralf describes how his company helps train what he calls robots. In other words, Ralf helps robots to see and hear by providing labelled data.

Kieran talked about data labelling as humans giving meaning to patterns. He explains that machines excel at finding patterns in data but that this data is only zeroes and ones to a machine. The patterns the machine finds are transformed into a mathematical formula but to a machine, these patterns are still only numbers. For Kieran, data labellers are central because they provide meaning to those numbers and, by extension, those patterns. As such, it is humans who provide meaning to the patterns that exist within data and it is often data labellers who provide this meaning.

Data-labelling companies not only employ experts in machine learning and those who label data but also many other specialisms. Larra, for instance, who works on designing virtual online assistants or chatbots, talks about the fact that in order to develop and sell such technologies, one requires not only data scientists and AI developers but a range of different disciplines. This is a point that was echoed by other interviewees like Georgia. Brenda herself was trained as a linguist and now works in data labelling. Brenda mobilised her identity as a linguist as opposed to a computer scientist when saying that a computer scientist would be happy with feeding a system enough data to ensure that it performs well enough. Her question is rather 'why does it work' and what information is being given to the system to train it. For her, data labelling helps to make AI more human-like.

For instance, an AI might interact with users in a human-like way if the data has been labelled in a specific way. To abstract from that, what Brenda is implying here is that data labelling allows AI to see the world like humans see the world. This is fundamentally a construction exercise where humans label data of how they see the world to allow AI to build a world that is replicating this human world.

Ava uses a similar way to express the need for data labelling. Ava explained that data labelling is an essential part of classifying which gives a computer the ability to understand the world in bits of data. However, she states that this is only 'noise' until a label is added. In order for the process of learning to begin, a label has to be attached to a pixel or a waveform through human input. For instance, the computer needs to learn that such a waveform corresponds to the word 'pet' and that this pixel is a cat. For Ava, supervised learning 'scaffolds' machine learning. It is interesting that Ava uses 'scaffolding' here, which is regularly used in regard to human learning (Wood et al., 1976). Ava then goes on to explain that in unsupervised learning, the machine finds features in the world on its own and aggregates those and puts labels onto them that might not correspond to human labels. This might contribute to what Ava calls black box issues around AI, in that AI leads to outputs that humans cannot follow. However, Ava describes this as fascinating because this is how AI can diverge from how humans see the world.

One of the machine learning experts, Darryl, provides an example of how humans and machines might diverge: a picture showing two humans running away from a hurricane on a beach would be identified by humans as a catastrophic image. Yet, the computer vision system has identified the image as two people hanging out on the beach. For Darryl, that shows the limitations of computer vision systems because the computer does not fully comprehend what is happening in that picture. The computer is missing the broader context. The machine lacks, as Kieran might express it, the meaning of patterns.

To summarise, the need for data labelling in machine learning can best be described as a way to help machines see and hear the world to make predictions based on this construction. If data labels are added by humans in supervised learning, the machine learns to see and hear the world from a human perspective. If data labels are added in unsupervised learning, the machine might construct a world that diverges from how humans see the world. In any case, machine learning is a way in which a world is constructed and as such, machine learning constructs a reality. Each construction of reality is going to be partial and subjective, as we will explore in the next section.

How Subjective Decisions Become Objective

In order to explore how subjective decisions in relation to data are transformed into something objective, it is useful to start with an explanation of how data labelling might work. Ava, who worked for a company providing data labelling, described how she would commonly work with engineers from the client side who specify what they need from the training data. She provides the example that a client might want speech data of 500 speakers with demographic diversity in regard to gender and dialect. Often, the client seeks advice on issues such as which dialects they should include for a specific language. The client also specifies the data structure, if data needs to be transcribed and the specific labels they need for their system to 'ingest' the data. Ingesting reflects what the system is expecting in terms of data. Ava explains that for speech recognition, they might use unintelligible tags that include filler words and coughs. The computer, according to Ava, needs to be able to distinguish a cough from a speech noise. This process of setting labels is normally a back and forth where the data-annotating company is suggesting certain labels or specific changes to labels.

I prompt Ava to talk more about who designs labels. She says that it really depends on the client, who sometimes has done labelling before, sometimes they need additional labels or they have an industry standard to comply with. In some cases, for instance, if the client is new to AI, the client might also seek advice on what labels to use. This then enables the data-labelling company to suggest some labels. Overall, Ava said that labels for automated speech recognition are often pretty standard. She stresses that the model is driving how labelling is done: what the computer needs to discriminate between data points is what drives labelling. She also talked about named entity recognition, which includes a standard set of labels such as organisation, person, location and nationality, among others. However, that differs from domain to domain. In the legal domain, for instance, different entities are required. Overall, she summarises that it depends on the final use case and what needs to be modelled that determines which labels are needed.

Similarly, Ralf stressed that his data annotation company is working closely with clients in developing labels. Some clients write the labels themselves or they want to use the technology, and thus, the labels that the data-annotating company provides. Ralf also states that sometimes the client formulates a problem where they ask the data-annotating company to help and train the client, which can then include instruction sets.

When talking about how labels are added, Raymond describes how the choice of which labels to include is meaningful. There are a range of labels available that are 'off the shelf' but which labels are being included in an algorithm is, in a sense, a choice. Joseph talks about ways in which meaning is imposed onto labels. What meaning is imposed onto a label is, as Joseph suggests, not objective but often deeply subjective. As a consequence, Joseph argues that the emerging labels are political in that they entail specific views of seeing the world. Kieran explains how those ways of seeing the world enter data labelling. Kieran suggests that those who design the labels have the power to determine what data labellers actually label. He provides the example that if a client in Northern Europe insists that all fruits that look like oranges should be labelled as apples, these are the instructions given to data labellers, who then label all oranges as apples in spite of the fact that they might see the fruit as an orange. Kieran argues that data labellers reproduce the views that clients want, with little room to challenge those views.

While Ralf thinks that instruction sets that include descriptors of different labels are important, he insists that the most crucial issue is the quality of the data that has to be tested. If an instruction is well-written but not tested, Ralf states that you still end up with 'garbage data'. Ava also talked about how it is useful to have a pilot phase to assess how well the labels are working for machine learning. Sometimes, it is also required to retrain the annotators and transcribers to use labels or to break something into two categories or even change categorisations altogether, according to Ava.

Since the quality of the data seems to be pivotal to the success of a data-labelling project, I asked Ralf how the quality of data is assured. Ralf explained that one way is to label the same data three times and check if one is statistically different to the other two. There are also reviewers who check the labelling for ten data labellers but that such reviews can increase if the task is more complex. They also use 'gold sets', which is data that is seen as correct, and compare the gold set to what the labeller has labelled. These gold sets are either provided by the customer or created in collaboration with the customer. Additionally, sometimes clients ask for audits of the people who do the data labelling to ensure that they are happy with the diversity among data labellers for a project.

In regard to how disagreements between labellers are handled, Ava explains that sometimes, if labellers disagree, they are not actually wrong as such but the guidelines favour one interpretation over the other. This illustrates the subjective nature of many of those decisions. According to Ava, there are two resolutions for this. Either the data labeller is encouraged to go back to the guidelines to correct how labels are assigned or it goes to an expert reviewer or arbitrator who makes the final decision. Ava describes this process as 'arbitrational curation', where a third person looks at the labelling and makes a final call. Another process for quality assurance relates to a sample review where a random 10% of the annotations is checked and feedback provided to the annotator, as Ava explains. If a systematic problem such as an inconsistency is uncovered, the remainder of the data is then fixed. Ava also talked about inter-annotator metrics, which is a tool to measure the difference in the labelling that different people do. The benchmark for this Ava names as Cohen's kappa. Cohen's kappa is a statistic that evaluates inter-rater reliability, or in other words, it measures the agreement of two raters. According to Ava, a Cohen's kappa of 0.8 and over is perfect or excellent agreement, which, as Ava stresses, is difficult to achieve. Ava mentioned that it is important to ensure early on that there is as much agreement as possible and to check throughout the process to ensure that there is no 'drift'. It can, for instance, happen that people see different examples and end up making different decisions on labels, which has to be corrected. Another way to ensure the quality that Ava talked about is to let three annotators label at least 20% of the data and then calculate Krippendorff's alpha, which is another statistic to evaluate inter-rater reliability, to measure agreement.

For Ava, one of the key quality measures is what she calls consensus. This consensus has to be agreed among a small group of data labellers. She also stresses that manual adjudication is used to deliver the final 'gold standard' decision. She describes this arbitration process as a negotiation because different perspectives are present and are brought together. It is not simply going with the majority but rather looking at the different perspectives and bringing them together. However, these perspectives come from a small number of people who do the annotation, which, for Ava, shows the importance of the diversity of those people doing the annotation. She compares this to a syntactic annotation task where what is a noun and what is a verb is not controversial, but someone might understand better than another person what a noun and a verb is. In this case, an agreement is probably not harmful. However, in sentiment annotation, Ava suggests that this is different because there is much more subjectivity and there is more diversity in the way that people understand sentiment. A similar point was raised by Nicole, who mentioned how those who label data often subjectively decide if someone in a picture looks happy or sad, in spite of the fact that little is known about how the person in the picture actually felt in that moment. Thereby, a data labeller might impose their reading of an emotion onto data, which she suggests is subjective. As such, there are labelling decisions that are more objective than others, with defining nouns and verbs being more objective but analysing sentiment being more subjective. Ava suggests that if we leave subjective decisions to a small range of people who might not be very diverse, this might impact decision.

Overall, in spite of the fact that the decisions of how to label data are highly codified through descriptions and regularly checked for quality, how a data labeller decides to label data might be a subjective interpretation and an act of meaning making. There are differences between people who label data but there might also be differences in how the same person labels data differently early in the week and late in the week. In some cases, the labels might be tightly defined, leaving little room for data labellers to include their views of the world in the data. In other instances, such as with sentiment analysis, there is more room for data labellers for subjective decision-making. The idea that an agreement or consensus can be reached in the form of gold sets or gold standard decisions encapsulates the idea that subjective decisions can be objectified if just the correct process is followed. Yet, ultimately, the decisions are made by humans and as such, these decisions are subjective.

Chains of Knowing about the World

So far, we have seen how subjective decisions are constructed as objective in regard to data for machine learning. I now want to expand this argument by looking at how a specific way of knowing about the world is embedded in data sets. Selena, for instance, talked about data sets not just materialising out of thin air but that are 'built by people who make decisions'. She goes on to explain that we think of data sets as 'objective sources of truth', which she finds concerning. She explains that categorisations and classifications have been custom-made for a context and are thus not universally applicable. Selena stresses that the context in which decisions on data sets are being made is important, and she suggests that there should be a record of these decisions. Selena goes further by stating that we also need to ask who is benefiting from this work. She argues that power dynamics that are embedded in data labelling need to be considered alongside the limitations of such data practices.

Darryl follows a similar line of thought when articulating how a machine learning practitioner might go about doing an image classification task. This process starts by conceptualising and framing what the task is and what labels might be used in the system, which is similar to what was discussed in the previous section. However, Darryl stresses that this involves deciding on a categorical schema based on which the millions of images that have been collected can be organised. Darryl suggests that there are a ton of design decisions that go into that, down to which words one uses to describe the world and in which language that is going to be. You might decide on English, which is then a Global North bias. Then you decide to pick a thousand words, but carving up the world into neat categories with limited words is not easy. Darryl states that perspectives shape this right down to which images show up in the data set in the first place. For instance, one might use a web search for the different categories such as doctor. Then there might be a human-in-the-loop, a data labeller, who says if this image shows a doctor. This collection of data is not perspectiveless, as Darryl states, because a person might have a specific conceptualisation of how a doctor, a nurse or, for the sake of the argument, a basketball, looks. The perspective that is taken, Darryl explains, is often a white male, Western perspective of the world.

Darryl goes on to stress that the choice of categories has a profound impact on machine learning and what categories machine learning is producing. These categories have to be linked to the 'signals' in the image. For example, if the data set only contains white, male doctors but no one in a surgeon's uniform or scrubs because that has not been labelled in the data, this has implications for what the system can 'see'. These data sets are, as Darryl stresses, not only used to train the AI system but also to assess its performance in the real world. This leads to a circular logic, as Darryl explains: if one uses a specific conceptualisation of what a doctor is and what a nurse is, this conceptualisation is used to measure how well the system works. Additionally, there is a specific conceptualisation of an image classification embedded in the data set; what is contained in an artificially fixed category is only one interpretation of the image. Darryl states that human vision is contextual in that how humans understand and describe the world depends on social identities and cultural contexts. Quenna raised a similar concern when she talked about how meaning is context dependent and will vary globally. In other words, not everyone is reading an image in the same way, but Darryl says that for machine learning, the human ways of interpreting the visual world are bounded and limited in regard to data sets. Darryl states that this has broad implications because the assumption is that computers can see and reveal the truth about an image. What Darryl is suggesting is that only specific ways of seeing are embedded in classifications and categorisations through which AI systems see the world.

Darryl expands on this point by talking about epistemology, which is underlying the construction of data sets. Darryl states that the underlying epistemology is that data labelling is about recognising a self-evident truth in an image. This resonates with how Callum described ground truth: an 'atomic bit of truth from the real world'. The assumption here is that the label assigned is a true representation of how the world is. Raymond, in contrast, talks about the ground truth of a data set as a better expression because what is described is what is correct within the data set. He stresses that this is not a general or generic truth or what might be true for one person, but rather a relationship within data.

Darryl, however, states that how this truth is established draws on processes, which are deemed to identify the obvious and self-evident. Crowd workers are expected to label images, and this process entails identifying something that is clear and obvious in the world and that crowd work is an acceptable way of solving that task. This has consequences, according to Darryl, for how this work is done, and that a faceless and nameless crew of workers who label images with average scores is an acceptable way of getting to this self-evident truth.

Darryl acknowledges that there are contextual differences in how people label. Darryl states that the facelessness and namelessness of this process also contributes to the impression of the final data sets being universal. However, Darryl questions if this universality is really true because it might be based on a single label attached to a single data instance. However, where this label came from and who ended up doing this work is lost. Darryl explains that this claim to universality is reflected in that the people doing the labelling are seen as not mattering. Those people are not seen, there are nameless, and where those people come from does not matter. It is accepted that a human has to do this work, but Darryl states that these infrastructures used to complete this work make workers invisible. To sum up thus far, Darryl connects the claim to universality of data that is made directly to the invisibility of workers. Only if the workers and the work are made invisible is it possible to claim that data labelling creates universal truths about the world.

Darryl then goes on to articulate how people have started to think about how different annotators bring different perspectives to bear, which needs to be captured. This can be variation in data labelling, which is a sign that people do a task differently. However, that is not the norm in data annotation because most data-labelling projects treat labels as self-evident, without the need of interpretation. Such variations in seeing need to be made invisible to ensure that data labels are efficient, scalable and cost-effective. In order to avoid that, Darryl suggests that it is necessary to recognise that ways of seeing the world differ among people.

The construction of ways of seeing and describing the world that both Selena and Darryl talk about is meaningful, not only for the working conditions in which such work is done, but it also ignores the fact that how people perceive and describe the world varies. While Ava recognised this point, Selena and Darryl expand on this and Darryl links it to epistemology. Ways of knowing differ and often, the perspectives that claim universality are in fact nothing but a god trick, as Haraway (1991) might say. There are specific perspectives embedded in how classifications are designed, how labels are described and how labels are being applied. However, most data sets seem to pretend that they offer a view from nowhere to claim that the information they entail is universally true. This in turn renders the mechanisms of production of these data sets invisible.

If a perspective is taken to represent the universal truth, this is possibly the perspective of designers of AI who develop the classifications and write the labels descriptions. The data annotators follow those instructions and, if they do not apply the labels correctly, are told how to label the world in ways that is described in the labels. However, data annotation companies have a crucial mediating function here. This is often considered in regard to what working conditions they offer. However, the data annotation companies also negotiate meaning between the data labellers and the AI designers in the client companies. This important mediating function of how knowledge is created remains often similarly unacknowledged. In other words, data-labelling companies are the organisational link in the epistemological chain – they mediate what knowing about the world is embedded in data labelling.

Constructing Gender

The fact that gender is commonly labelled as a binary was regularly discussed by those who were involved in and familiar with data-labelling processes. A common concern raised by, for instance, Parker, Darryl and Ava is that gender in AI is typically binary. Ava asks what that would mean for a person who does not identify as one of those binary genders. Ava said that decisions are being made based on the categories that are included in an AI system. She thus alludes to the fact that those who do not identify based on the two options of gender offered, might not be included and thus become invisible. Selena similarly points to the problem of reifying gender through categorising people along a gender binary while also erasing trans and queer identities. Additionally, Selena is concerned that intersectional experiences of gender are made invisible. She explains that the experiences of a white woman are different from a Black woman and just lumping women into a category of women is making this difference invisible.

Brenda mentioned that more clients are concerned about bias in the data but that most of the data still follows a binary approach in regard to gender. Darryl also spoke about the assumption that gender is commonly conceptualised as a binary and that gender is treated as knowable from an image. Darryl explains that gender appears as a fixed and a natural category in machine learning, even though it is constructed, situated and shifting. This is problematic for the development of computer vision systems, as Darryl states. However, like Brenda, Darryl has observed a shift in recent years where it has been recognised that gender is not binary and that it is not possible to know someone's gender by looking at an image. Instead, if data sets are labelled with gender, the data is labelled with 'perceived gender'. Darryl asserts that this is a step in the right direction because most data sets have an asterisk next to gender with the statement that gender is not binary. Darryl says that this acknowledges the idea that gender is not a binary but she complains that the same data sets then go on to use gender as a binary. The same phenomenon of stating that gender is non-binary to proceed with gender conceptualised as a binary was observed by Parker. Such a discursive move shows that there is an awareness for gender as a non-binary, which, however, does not lead to any changes in practices of how gender is conceptualised.

Darryl states that even if data sets are labelled with perceived gender, these perceptions are still culturally and socially situated perceptions of masculine and feminine presentations. Darryl stresses that such perceptions shift geographically between cultures but also in regard to age and race. In Darryl's view, classifying people into gender categories is problematic because those categorisations are often racialised and could be seen as an expression of what Darryl calls a colonial project. Darryl says that who defines those categories of perceived male and perceived female is central because these are not objective or self-evident.

This raises wider questions for Darryl in regard to what needs to be measured at all. So, for instance, if you need a system that works for different gender categories, it might be best to go with self-identification of individuals. If one needs to know how a system performs for people with short or long hair, facial hair or not, then this could be used for analysis. If you need a gender label and cannot rely on self-identification, Darryl suggests that framing those labels as not self-evident is central and that going with the perception of labellers might be possible if this would be framed as a perception rather than a fact.

Darryl goes on to explain that the labellers could give some evidence why they come to a judgment, such as what a person is wearing, the perception of secondary sex characteristics, grooming styles or presentation. For Darryl, the articulation of how one arrives at a judgement is key and would allow contextualising the resulting labels. It has to be clear that these are judgements, not an objective measure. According to Darryl, part of the problem is how questions to data labellers are formulated. Furthermore, as Darryl states, one has to collect information about the data labellers themselves because people who have different relationships with gender, such as being queer, trans or gender-diverse folk,[4] might come to different judgements in regard to gender labels than a cisgender person who has never thought about the socially constructed nature of gender. A similar point was raised by Hayden. Additionally, people from different cultures might understand gender categories differently, as Darryl points out. Darryl states that it is therefore important what informs their reading of gender and why they read gender in certain ways. Such additional information about data labellers alongside framing questions in a precise fashion will allow for annotations that are contextualised.

Another reason why labelling gender might be important is provided by Callum. Callum talked about the risk of categories being inferred, which he constructs as more problematic than having an explicit label. He provides the example of someone who might have a LGBT[5] initiative on their CV. Then, according to Callum, it is not clear if you identify as LGBT or if you are an ally. However, for the model, that does not matter because it might still infer from the data that you are a less good candidate. Callum implies that if LGBT status would be explicitly labelled, there might be ways to mitigate for bias, which is more difficult if there is no label but the information is inferred. Similarly, Sabine stated that even when gender is not explicitly stated, there will be a plethora of proxies for gender that are inferred from data. This concern goes back to some issues that were discussed in Chapter 4.

Brenda provides a similar example when referring to an academic paper. The paper used language data from Trustpilot to analyse gender and word choice. Brenda is sceptical about the methodology used in the paper: not only was gender regarded as binary but names were used to deduct if a person is a woman or a man. The paper found that women and men use different words, with women being more descriptive, such as using fantastic, wonderful, awesome, happy, and men using words focusing on price and quality, like inexpensive, economic, cheap, best quality and so on. When I asked what this might mean, that an AI could conclude that by using such words you are a woman, Brenda provides a use case where a person writes a review about a product, the language is analysed, the person is classified as woman or man, according to the language used, and then the person is shown advertisements targeted at women. Brenda later expands on that by saying that language is part of gender socialisation and non-binary individuals might also use language in different ways and might thus not be targeted correctly by those ads.

Gender was also discussed in relation to language translations. Brenda talked about an example from Google Translate, where Hungarian is translated into English. Brenda shares an example with me where in Hungarian, the pronouns are gender neutral, but the English translation transforms this gender neutrality into something that is stereotypically gendered such as 'she is beautiful' and 'he is clever'. What is interesting is that the original language was not gendered but gendering is introduced when the text is translated. Here, the machine translation is doing the gendering. Brenda uses a specific example from developing a chatbot where the chatbot automatically was referenced as a he and the interior designer was referenced as a she.

Another issue in relation to gender is co-reference tagging. Co-reference tagging means, as Brenda explains, to tag the reference between names and pronouns. She uses the example, 'Alex went to the concert; he said it was amazing', which means that 'Alex' and 'he' are co-referent and 'concert' and 'it' are co-referent. But what happens if Alex is a woman? Then the system needs to be able to understand that Alex can be a 'she'. Or if Alex is non-binary then the system should say 'they'. Brenda says that if a system is not trained to have this flexibility, it is likely to exclude and the system is biased. However, Brenda acknowledges that she has never seen such a project that was designed with inclusion in mind.

Speech recognition might also pose specific challenges from a diversity perspective. Ava talked about how in speech data collection, one might attempt to find examples of regional dialects and then have men and women speak in that dialect, but the more granular this intersectionality becomes, the less examples there will be, which is also something Georgia mentioned. This affects the training data, which Ava says will be less robust.

Speech recognition also has a normative aspect to it, as Brenda elaborates. She states that automatic speech recognition voices like Siri and Alexa speak standard voices, emulating what is called stable linguistic periods of people. This period is defined as people between the ages of 20 and 55. Data sets might contain 10%–15% of people over 65, which might mean that people over 65 are less well understood. Equally younger people, who might be more innovative with language or who might or might not go through puberty, might also not be understood. The speech data will also be collected from men and women, and as such, trans persons might be less well understood. Similarly, what Brenda describes as 'stereotypical gay male speech' is something that an automation speech recognition engine needs to be trained on.

Finally, another issue relating to gender that was mentioned was that Siri and Alexa and other VPAs had default feminine-sounding voices (see also Chapter 1). This is a topic of regular academic, policy and media concern (Equals & UNESCO, 2019; Dillon, 2020; Strengers & Kennedy, 2020; Sutko, 2020), which has led providers to offer more diversity in VPA voices (Baraniuk, 2022). As such, it is not surprising that the topic was mentioned in the interviews as well. Ava suggested that the default feminine voices reflect gender stereotypes that designers had, but she also talked about how there are now attempts to develop non-binary voices, for instance, in Project Q – an attempt to create a genderless voice (Project Q, 2023).[6] While Ava thought that this is an interesting development, she wondered in how far this will remain niche and the standard is going to be feminine voices for assistants. Similarly, Larra talked about how many of her clients give virtual assistants or chatbots a gendered and often feminine name. She describes how she is pushing back against clients who pick gendered names and she proudly states that most of the virtual assistant or chatbots she worked on did not end up with gendered names.

Overall, many of the interviewees articulate how gender is relevant for data labelling and, by extension, machine learning. The interviewees showed an awareness for the fact that current practices around gender and data often mean that binary gender is reified. While many described these processes as problematic, they also acknowledged how difficult it is to change those practices towards more inclusion. Moreover, it is evident that practices around data labelling are constructing gender. The gender patterns used in machine learning shape which gender patterns are predicted.

Conclusion

The chapter focused on patterns that humans have to recognise to help AI learn. This chapter started with the question of how machines recognise gender patterns, or in other words, how a machine knows who is a woman, a man or non-binary. The chapter suggested that machines perceive the world through labels that are assigned by humans or developed during machine learning. If humans add these labels, this often happens through AI's hidden workforce – those who label data as a crowd work task or by individuals adding labels working in the AI supply chain. This work is often done in the Global South. While much research has rightly focused on the working conditions of these workers, this chapter has particularly stressed that such workers interpret the world but that these interpretations are made invisible. The chapter explains that data labelling is necessary to allow machine learning systems to recognise patterns, which then form part of the outputs the machine produces, or in other words, the predictions. Therefore, data labelling is needed for AI to help machines see, hear and understand the world. For this to happen, a ground truth – labelled data that is assumed to be true in machine learning – needs to be established to allow machine learning and to check the quality of machine learning.

Labels are classifications and the chapter discusses how classifications are ways in which the world is ordered. It was shown that once this organisation of knowledge has happened, the classifications often become accepted for how the world is. As such, these ways of organising the world through classifications such as in machine learning labels are political but the processes of construction are made invisible. In data labelling, it is seen as important to create a consensus among human labellers and moderators about which labels to apply to best represent the world. These processes entail turning subjective decisions into a seemingly objective and universal truth. However, the chapter has shown that this universality is carefully negotiated between different actors in data labelling who embed what is knowable about the world in labelled data sets. What is knowable about gender in data labelling generally seems to follow an understanding of gender as a binary, with limited scope to conceive gender beyond a binary. The world that is being constructed through machine learning is in many ways a simplified understanding of the world, which is presented as objective and universal. Thereby, classifications that are conceptualised and operationalised through data labels construct a reality. Yet, this construction of reality is a potentially exclusionary one. Building more inclusionary approaches in regard to data labelling is central to make these construction processes visible and tangible. As such, the chapter has argued that there are some patterns that only humans can recognise but that the subjective processes based on which this recognition happens are regularly made invisible to suggest that these patterns are objective and universal.

Notes

1 Data labelling and data annotation are used interchangeably in this chapter.
2 It should be noted that academic research often relies on MTurk as well (Aguinis et al., 2021). For example, academic research regularly draws on MTurk to find participants who can complete surveys.
3 Sama says it offers premium pay and psychological support for such type of work (Perrigo, 2023). Yet, it has been claimed that such psychological support is difficult to access (Perrigo, 2023).
4 This is the terminology Darryl used.
5 LGBT is the term Callum used.
6 Project Q aims to create a genderless voice and should not be confused with OpenAI's Q* project (Lee, 2023).

6

CONCLUSION

UNWRITTEN RULES

Introduction

In this final chapter, I will bring the different threads in regard to gender and digitalisation in the future of work together to show which patterns emerge. I illustrate how the individual aspects that were explored through the book are connected to one another and form specific patterns in which gender and digitalisation are said to unfold. The book has shown how certain versions of the future are constructed. These futures can be more or less desirable in that they oscillate between utopian and dystopian visions of the future. The book was centrally concerned with which patterns these imagined futures assume. The book traces which jobs are constructed as endangered by automation and which jobs are constructed as safe from automation. The book highlighted how ideal future employees are predicted using technologies and how certain subjectivities are created by how AI is designed, while others are made invisible. The underlying concern of this book was to understand how gender from an intersectional perspective matters in these processes. These future-making practices are productive in that they create possibilities for how futures might unfold. The book drew

DOI: 10.4324/9781003427100-6

on material that was generated to speak to a variety of contexts in which the dynamics between gender and digitalisation can be expected to be particularly pronounced. I conducted interviews with experts on the future of work, with individuals who could comment on changes in professional work, with people working on AI in hiring and training, and with those who work on data, data labelling and AI. These contexts appear as distinct and different, yet through the analysis presented in the book, I was able to show that these contexts are not only individually highly relevant for understanding gender and digitalisation in the future of work but taken together, specific patterns form that are likely to shape futures of work in relation to gender and digitalisation. I thus argue in this book that the patterns that emerge shape futures of work for gender and digitalisation, and only by taking them together can we understand the complex and dynamic connections between digitalisation and gender. At the centre of this chapter are how the individual threads explored throughout the book form patterns that are meaningful for understanding gender and digitalisation in the work context.

Predicting Futures and Imagining Alternative Futures

Knowing what the future will hold is a central human need (Nowotny, 2021). As the future is yet to be, we rely on predictions of what these futures might hold. These predictions can – like in the case of AI – be based on data. They might also be based on creative imagination. While one might be tempted to see predictions based on data as objective and creative imagination as subjective, this book has shown that futures based on predictions emerging from data and on creative imagination are socially constructed. In other words, which groups of individuals an author of a book on the future of work foregrounds is as much a social construction as which skills are deemed important for a job selection and evaluated in AI-supported hiring. These constructions are the results of choices that are made and these choices have consequences. They might influence where attention is paid or it might influence who finds future employment. An individual thread might carry little relevance, yet many different threads woven together form specific patterns. Similarly, each individual social construction might appear as carrying little relevance, but as a collective, they form patterns that can include or exclude. These patterns are social: they emerge from social relations and, simultaneously, shape them.

The book has advanced the argument that the imagination of the future is meaningful because it shapes potential trajectories that the future might take. Where emphases are placed and what is included in those visions of the future matters for which routes are taken. As such, exploring how the future of work is imagined in books on that topic and how experts talk about this future (see Chapters 2 and 3) creates an idea of what is in focus and what is left out of focus. The underlying idea is that futures are socially constructed and what is foregrounded and what is ignored is central to those shaping processes. It also allows for creating the potential of alternative visions of those futures that might ensure that those futures are fairer and more equal than the present.

If futures are socially constructed in and through technology, then this also allows for creating alternative futures. In Chapter 2, I have shown how the man-versus-machine trope is regularly mobilised to illustrate the dangers of technology. The trope is attractive because it has long been established and endlessly recycled from movies to newspaper headlines. However, we can create alternative imaginations by, for instance, showing how the generic man is far from generic; for example, a Black man is positioned differently to an Asian man in regard to such technologies. While it should be avoided to homogenise humans and to instead show their diversity, the same is true for machines. Machines are not homogeneous. They have, in a sense, diversity too. As such, it is important to raise awareness for diversity among humans and among machines. This can then create novel reflections and alternative pathways of how futures might unfold that can be more inclusive. Similarly, if the generic middle-class professional is exposed as a white man, this can aid in creating awareness that professional jobs are more diverse than we commonly assume.

Whereas drudgework was constructed as replaceable by machines, socio-emotional skills were regularly constructed as uniquely human (see Chapter 3). Yet, it was implied but rarely discussed that it is largely women who use socio-emotional skills in care work.[1] The common response is to stress that the socio-emotional skills that women display need to be recognised, valued and rewarded (Kelan, 2008a). However, in this book, I have encouraged an alternative vision of the future where socio-emotional skills can be performed by machines because they follow specific patterns that can be automated. As such, these skills are not uniquely human and do not constitute a competitive advantage of humans over machines. We need to imagine and thus prepare for futures where socio-emotional skills are performed with and through machines. Moreover, we need to reflect on which socio-emotional skills should be performed by humans, not due to the fact that machines cannot display such skills but rather because we prefer those skills to be performed by humans.

In Chapter 4, I traced how algorithmic bias in hiring is constructed as a technical problem, which can be fixed through technology. Thereby, the problem of discrimination, inequality and exclusion is positioned as fixable through technology. This contributes to the fiction that societal issues can be remedied through technology. While I can certainly see the potential of technology to make discrimination visible, as I suggest in this chapter, my point here is to consider how technology is presented as a solution to societal problems without considering that a technology is always both reflecting and shaping social relations. An alternative vision for the future is to then understand technology as social, which can create exclusion but might equally well also pave the way to inclusion, depending on which decisions are made when technology is developed and used. As such, I have suggested that we need to create more awareness for the social shaping of technology rather than accepting technology as a solution to societal problems like exclusion.

The book also pointed to the mechanisms of production as central for how exclusion and inclusion are being created through technologies (see Chapter 5). How inclusive the worlds created through AI are depends on how these worlds are constructed. I have argued that it is vital to highlight which knowledges enter processes around machine learning and that these knowledges have to be understood as situated rather than a view from nowhere (Haraway, 1991). Visions of such futures need to make the situatedness of these knowledges visible. Equally, attention has to be paid to what is being excluded though such production processes. For instance, we need to reflect on how intersectional subjectivities can be reflected in data and resulting AI constructions.

Patterns of Inclusion and Exclusion

The book has traced patterns of inclusion and exclusion. We have seen in Chapters 2 and 3 how imagining the future has effects on who is potentially included and excluded in those futures of work. These patterns of inclusion and exclusion were also central in regard to how hiring technologies can foster or hinder diversity (see Chapter 4). Equally, how specific knowledges are ignored or made invisible is relevant in relation to data labelling (see Chapter 5). Much of the underlying technology is reading patterns in data to project this data into the future and thus repeating and amplifying these patterns (Nowotny, 2021). If these patterns are exclusionary, then the emerging futures are likely to exclude as well. Similarly, if these patterns are inclusive, consequently, there is the potential for futures to be inclusive.

However, these patterns of exclusion and inclusion are complex and dynamic. Although examples of how AI is creating exclusion are attracting regular media and academic attention, what is being reported and discussed is likely only a fraction of how exclusion is perpetuated through technologies. Many of the technologies are proprietary and will thus not be accessible to the wider public. The wider public will simply not hear about many of those instances where technologies repeat patterns of exclusion (Crawford, 2021). Similarly, the focus on punctual and sporadic stories that emerge in the media and some academic research disguises how inclusion is created through some technologies. For example, in regard to hiring, some of the interviewees I spoke to had limited awareness of how their technologies could exclude. If these technologies were shown to be exclusionary, some of those who sell these technologies even used this as free publicity to sell their technology (see Chapter 4). Even though the company might be in the media because it repeats exclusion, it still provided essentially free advertising to the company. However, in other organisations, concerns around exclusion were used as a way to improve the technology developed. Although much of this followed the idea that it is possible to fix algorithmic bias (see Chapter 4), the underlying concern was to create patterns of inclusion. This means that the emerging patterns are more complex and dynamic than commonly assumed.

Academics and the media often gravitate towards patterns of exclusion. These patterns are attractive because they make good stories. In the media, they might create engagement of readers. For academics, the suspicion that technologies are questionable is confirmed. These narratives are in a way expected and predictable. They are expected and predictable because in the development and use of technology, elements around diversity and inclusion are rarely major concerns. It is thus important for the media and academia to showcase examples of where exclusion is created to potentially inspire more inclusive practices. In my interviews, I was able to document a few instances where negative reporting has indeed created and supported efforts to develop more inclusive practices around the design and use of technologies.

Yet, examples of how inclusion can be created in and through technologies are few and far between. The reason for this is in part that it is more straightforward to spot exclusion than it is to develop practices and processes that foster inclusion. For example, I found in my earlier research that it is easier to document examples of where gender exclusion happens than to show how inclusion can be created (Kelan, 2015, 2023a). It is then not surprising that in regard to technologies, documenting exclusion is more straightforward than showing how inclusion might be generated. In this book, I thus attempted to focus both on the practices of exclusion and those of inclusion. The emerging pattern is a more dynamic one than one often presumes. For instance, organisations that attempt to create technologies that include different people find that there are unintended consequences. If facial recognition is excluded, the words individuals chose might still indicate the gender they identify with (see Chapter 4). The social nature of data was also mentioned in Chapter 5. The book has thus shown that data is social and will reflect the society from which it emerged.

If data is understood as social, it is possible to trace society through these patterns but it also makes creating inclusion a more difficult endeavour. As I have argued in Chapter 4, seeing algorithmic bias as something that can be fixed through technical means neglects that technology is reflective of society and *vice versa*. This means that fixing technology is more complicated than simply flipping a switch. It requires approaches that entail a deep understanding of society. The solutions to technical problems cannot be delivered through technical solutions but require the knowledge of those who know about the social. Technology companies therefore add anthropologists or poets to design teams (Daugherty & Wilson, 2018) (see also Chapter 2). Those individuals are presumed to help those companies engaging with the social. However, one could argue that it is equally important to ensure that AI designers have an understanding of how the technologies they design reflect and shape society and that this is embedded in respective curricula.

From Magic to Making Rules Visible

For many people, terms like AI, algorithms or digitalisation appear mythical and magical because the workings of those technologies are hidden from sight (Finn, 2017) (see also Chapter 1). Similarly, the term 'black box' describes the opaqueness of technologies where even those who design these new technologies can often not fully explain why they work in specific ways (Pasquale, 2015). In Chapter 5, I have argued that invisibilities around how data is prepared for AI are central to make AI appear as objective and universal. However, these invisibilities of such processes are also important to see AI as magical and mythical. This magical and mythical nature of technologies invites us to engage with these technologies in ritualistic ways that can function to mitigate the risks and uncertainties of modern life (Finn, 2017). While those technologies might provide a kind of ritualistic comfort, many of those technologies have consequences for people's lives and as such, there is an urgent need to understand and explain how these technologies work. In a sense, it is important to make technologies less magical and mythical to start engaging with them in a more enlightened way.

Throughout the book, I have suggested that technology is shaped in design and use by society and *vice versa*. This perspective emerges from the social shaping of technology approach (MacKenzie & Wajcman, 1999) (see Chapter 1). Research in this vein would normally show how specific technologies are shaped by society, such as how the electric version of the refrigerator became the norm (Cowan, 1999). Another example comes from the gendered meanings associated with microwave ovens. When the microwave was first introduced into homes, it was imagined and marketed as a way for men to reheat food but its usage often led to unexpected results such as women customising individual meals for family members with the aid of a microwave (Cockburn & Ormrod, 1993). This classical study about gender and technology highlights the fluctuating and interrelated ways in which meaning around new technologies intersects with gender (Cockburn & Ormrod, 1993). Such studies above all show how social relations enter technology; social norms enter the design and use of technologies and these technologies shape social norms in turn. Technologies such as AI learn social norms through data but also associated processes and decisions (see Chapters 4 and 5). As such, these technologies are learning the unwritten rules of society. But these technologies will also be able to pick up changes and inconsistencies in relation to such patterns. For instance, the research on microwave ovens shows how gender materialises in technology in expected but also unexpected ways, leading to patterns that show continuity but also change (Cockburn & Ormrod, 1993). So far, research has largely focused on the patterns that repeat exclusion, such as by creating algorithmic biases and as such, automating inequalities (Eubanks, V., 2018). However, one can expect that there is possibly more variety in the patterns of inclusion and exclusion that emerge in relation to gender and digitalisation.

Although AI and related technologies are rightly seen as creating risks of exclusion (Eubanks, V., 2018; Benjamin, 2019), I have discussed traces of how AI-supported hiring can be understood as making the underlying rules of society visible and thus tangible (see Chapter 4). In Chapter 4, I showed how those who design and use hiring technologies construct algorithmic bias as ultimately fixable. I have critiqued this perspective as an expression of techno-optimism that conceives society as something that is fixable through technological means. Such a perspective permeates the tech industry. This techno-optimism suggests that the black box of technology can be opened and corrective measures can be taken, leading to explainable AI. I questioned if such biases are fixable because they are a function of society. However, while the idea of a technological fix of societal issues should be questioned, technologies such as AI afford us with the possibility of showing how the unwritten rules in society function to systematically exclude groups of people. AI as a pattern reader and repeater is central to understanding the unwritten rules of how societies operate. In other words, AI repeats and amplifies human biases but it also makes inequalities that exist in society visible. However, there is nothing mere about this because crystallising the unwritten rules of society is important and meaningful.

Making the unwritten rules of society visible is meaningful, not in the sense that it allows us to apply a technical fix, as many of the interviewees suggested. Instead, it might allow us to change the unwritten rules of society in general and at scale. For example, previous interventions in regard to discrimination in the workplace have focused on 'fixing' individual decision-makers. If a white male hiring manager ends up hiring a younger version of himself, we tried to change the practices of the individual manager by calling out this pattern.[2] Hypothetically, AI-supported hiring technologies might now show us that white, young men might be generally the preferred candidate to be hired. For other positions such as in care work, the implicit assumption might be that such work is done by women from the Global South. This is of course something that researchers have shown for a long time (Acker, 1990). In fact, we have seen in Chapter 2 that many discourses on the future of work contain a concern for a specific type of person: male, white-collar professionals. This was the implicit ideal worker imagined in the books on the future of work. AI has the potential to make such unwritten rules visible and tangible in a systematic way. Although I would caution against attempting to fix society by fixing technology, being able to make the unwritten rules tangible might allow for changing them as societies.

Such a perspective also opens the possibility of seeing such patterns as more complex and dynamic. There might be dominant and less dominant patterns but there might also be patterns that contradict each other. This complexity and dynamic nature of pattern is central to how societies function, and stressing such contradictions and complications in patterns would be a novel way to think about digitalisation and gender. There are always multiple patterns competing for attention. Equally, for new patterns to form, a new component needs to be introduced or emphasised. We have seen a moment of such a recognition in relation to the wild card hires in Chapter 4. If we hire people who might not fit the pattern in the most perfect way, we open up the opportunity for new patterns to emerge. As such, patterns should not be seen as determinist. Such perspectives dominate thinking on algorithmic bias where the risk of repeating past patterns is leading to exclusion. While such risks have to be taken seriously, it is also important to remember that new patterns can be created, which might lead to greater inclusion.

As a matter of fact, the common fix to algorithmic bias, fixing the data, is in a sense introducing a new pattern. Since data is often constructed as the basis for algorithmic bias, as we have seen in Chapter 4, many approaches to deal with algorithmic bias are centred on fixing the data. This might include ensuring that data sets represent society. If AI fails to recognise Black faces, the solution is to include more Black faces from which AI can learn (Buolamwini & Gebru, 2018). If AI suggested only male candidates because the underlying data set included largely men's CVs, then the solution is to include CVs by women (Dastin, 2018). Chapter 4 details many of those 'fixes' to ensure that algorithmic bias is reduced. We also need to look at how data is being produced and processed, which was at the centre of Chapter 5. It has been suggested that ways forward are datasheets for data sets (Gebru et al., 2021). Datasheets should include, for instance, information about the motivation to collect this data, the composition of the data set, the collection process of the data, the pre-processing/cleaning/labelling of the data set, uses, distribution and maintenance (Gebru et al., 2021). By providing detailed questions that should be considered in datasheets for data sets, Gebru and co-authors (2021) provide admirable guidance to improve data sets.

While these approaches to improved data are necessary, it is questionable if they are sufficient. Data will be improved by being more representative, more ethical and more transparent. However, the underlying issue that data is reflecting society will remain. Outstanding data practices might help to reduce algorithmic bias, but the social patterning of data might come through in another way. For example, in AI-supported hiring, a provider might drop facial recognition to avoid that the selection of suggested candidates is not influenced by the technology being less able to recognise Black women. Yet, the same Black women might use certain language constructions, which might be judged as less suitable for a role and thus filtered out. Of course, good data practices could reduce these risks, but there is a danger that algorithmic biases emerge in other shapes and forms because data is inherently social. Societal relations imprint on data. However, as I have argued, it is also possible to use this as an opportunity to create alternative patterns.

Reification Machines

Reification is a charge regularly levied against research on gender. For instance, research might state that gender is seen as socially constructed, yet then proceeds in the empirical part to operate based on a fixed gender binary (Nentwich & Kelan, 2014). For much research on gender, a standard criticism is that such research is re-establishing gender binaries rather than challenging them. Seeing gender as fluid and flexible to counteract the conception of gender as a fixed binary has been discussed in academia, at least since Butler's seminal book, *Gender Trouble* (Butler, 1990). The idea of gender beyond a binary has received purchase in wider society.[3] While such conceptions of gender are often derided as being part of 'gender ideology'

(Kuhar & Paternotte, 2017), it should be noted that, for example, Germany legally recognises a third gender and thus moves beyond a gender binary (Anti-Diskriminierungsstelle des Bundes, 2023). One could thus argue that moving beyond a gender binary, which has been central for gender studies for a while, is increasingly something that is recognised in organisations and wider society.

While moving beyond gender binaries has reached the mainstream, there is a strong tendency in AI to re-establish the gender binary. For example, in HR, attempts have been made to offer more than two options to signify gender, yet in AI-supported hiring, gender is largely treated as a binary (see Chapter 4). As I have shown in Chapter 5, the gender binary as underlying classification is rarely questioned in machine learning. Similar to research in gender studies, research in machine learning often states that gender is not a binary yet proceeds to treat gender as an unchangeable binary (Keyes, 2018) (see also Chapter 5). Machines read gender through the data in a variety of ways. Gender might be self-identified or someone else is picking a gender label. Furthermore, gender is embedded in data through, for instance, certain words that people commonly read as words women use. Even though popular perceptions of gender are moving beyond a gender binary, AI is often reifying gender as a binary.

If AI is a gender reification machine, this affords the ability to study the unwritten rules through which gender is established. Approaches that see gender as a doing (West & Zimmerman, 1987) or performed (Butler, 1990) often seek to understand such unwritten rules of how gender is established in interactions. For example, Goffman's (1979) work on advertising showed the ritualisation of gender by showing how relative size is a marker of gender. Garfinkel's (1984) work engaged with identifying markers of femininity. If AI is making rules of societal interactions visible, then AI is an opportunity to understand gender in society.

The emerging worlds of AI reify gender as a binary or, in other words, AI creates worlds that are by and large based on gender binaries. If gender is treated as a binary in daily life and data reflects this, machines will learn gender binaries by default. It has been rightly pointed out that this is problematic if it leads to individuals being misgendered (Keyes, 2018). It also restricts which futures can be developed. If we rely on AI replicating a certain version of society, this limits which futures can be created. In this case, futures where gender moved beyond a binary are less likely. As such, reifying gender in and through AI means that what futures are possible is curtailed.

Politics of Visibilities

An underlying concern for this book were processes of how gender is made visible and invisible in discourses on the future of work (Chapters 2 and 3) but also in relation to how AI constructs a specific reality (Chapter 5). As discussed in Chapter 2, in books on the future of work, the main concern was for male, middle-class breadwinners whose jobs might be automated. The common concern was that if machines take over jobs, people will not be able to earn an income. However, someone might still profit from the labour of machines: those who own the machines. For instance, these might be founders of or shareholders in Silicon Valley companies. We have also seen in Chapter 5 that the working practices of data labellers and how they contribute to constructing AI worlds are made invisible. One could even go as far to talk about epistemic erasure (Mahalingam & Selvaraj, 2023) in this context. The concept of epistemic erasure denotes a process of how the lived experiences of those from disadvantaged backgrounds are delegitimised through cultural practices shaped by privileged groups (Mahalingam & Selvaraj, 2023).[4] Moreover, most of these data labellers work indirectly for organisations that, through their labour, turn a profit. However, ownership structures and who profits from running the machines or from the efforts of data labellers are hidden from sight in most accounts on the future of work. The likelihood is that those who profit from the labour of machines belong to fairly small groups of individuals.

Concerns around the future of work manifest in tropes such as the epic battle between man and machine. During the First Industrial Revolution, physical power was replaced by machines and the assumption was that humans were superior intellectually (Standage, 2002). However, AI that appears to display human-like intelligence is now a major underlying concern driving the thinking on the future of work. Hence, we see those who have traditionally used their intellect to earn a living, such as professional workers, being the main focal point for concerns in regard to the future of jobs. These concerns are mitigated through two discursive strategies: first, to point towards augmentation to suggest that humans and machines collaborate and, as such, humans are required in the future; second, to suggest that certain abilities are beyond the realm of machines such as socio-emotional skills. Yet, as I have shown in Chapter 3, socio-emotional skills are within the realm of machines because they follow automatable patterns. This does not mean that machines have emotions but that they can read and respond to emotions that humans display. Like with other social interactions, machines can discern the unwritten rules of emotions from data and repeat these patterns to, for instance, train ideal emotional responses in humans. It appears that like during the Industrial Revolution, when physical power was replaced by machines but intelligence was perceived as uniquely human, technologies like AI seem to threaten human intelligence, yet imply that socio-emotional skills are uniquely human. However, this assumption might not hold true if machines also appear human-like in regard to emotions.

There are obvious tensions between becoming visible and being not visible. In some instances, gaining visibility is central for having one's identity recognised, yet in other cases, having personal data revealed can be harmful. Data is often scraped from the internet such as from social media, which can be used, for instance, in hiring. Scraping data from social media for hiring is problematic because it violates the privacy of candidates and might also reveal membership affiliations, such as in relation to age or race (Black et al., 2015; Jeske et al., 2019). Similarly, belonging to an LGBTQ group could lead to individuals being ranked lower in hiring processes (Tomasev et al., 2021). It has also been suggested that some data might be too sensitive to include. An example would be how Grindr passed users' HIV status to third parties; while this information is provided voluntarily and with consent, it has been suggested that this information is too sensitive to be held by such platforms (Rzepka, 2023). In such cases, visibility might be highly problematic because it can be used to exclude individuals.

Another way to deal with the invisibility of data is synthetic data (Eldan & Li, 2023; Gunasekar et al., 2023; Jacobsen, 2023). Synthetic data promises to provide unbiased and labelled data by including variation on, for instance, age, race and gender (Jacobsen, 2023). Given the complexity of real-life data for facial recognition, the Mixed Reality & AI Labs at Microsoft Cambridge developed the model ConfigNet to generate photorealistic synthetic faces, while allowing a modification of these outputs, for instance, by adopting different poses or including different skin tones (Jacobsen, 2023). As we have seen, for instance, in Chapter 4, the underlying data is often blamed for algorithmic bias, and synthetic data seems attractive because it eradicates issues around representation in data sets; in other words, if a group is underrepresented, the missing group is simply generated and then included in machine learning. Jacobsen (2023) warns of the tendency to solely see algorithmic bias as a 'training dataset problem' that can be fixed using synthetic data. Algorithmic bias can, as we have seen in Chapter 4, also emerge through designing models poorly (see also Jacobsen, 2023). Jacobsen (2023) argues that synthetic data is presented as a way to de-risk data where synthetic data is constructed as risk-free. However, such a move also means that wider criticism in regard to resisting and challenging machine learning is silenced (Jacobsen, 2023). Synthetic data can be seen as another way to 'fix' data and thus algorithm without paying attention to wider social implications of technologies (Jacobsen, 2023). As I have outlined earlier in this chapter, trying to exclude the social from data is highly problematic. Although synthetic data promises to resolve many issues in regard to diversity and inclusion, unless technology is understood as social, such fixes will remain partial.

Accountability and Responsibility

The book also offers perspectives on accountability and responsibility in relation to digitalisation. Throughout the book, I have stressed that technologies are shaped by social relations and *vice versa*, drawing on the social shaping of technology approach (MacKenzie & Wajcman, 1999). The book has provided countless examples of how this shaping happens, from how AI is used in hiring (Chapter 4) to how data is labelled for AI to learn (Chapter 5). The central idea emerging from material is that technology does not appear out of nowhere. It is created by people, and how these people think and behave influences what technology is created. Which technology is created is also influenced by those who finance the development of those technologies. As I have outlined in Chapter 1, there are vested interests behind fostering one technology over another. Such an ability to shape technologies also comes with responsibility and accountability.

While most research tends to show us how traditional social patterns are repeated, I suggested in this book that the potential of the social shaping of technology can be utilised to create, develop and foster technology that is creating more inclusive futures. This is not an automatic process but one that requires that care is taken of and consideration is given to how gender as well as other forms of diversity affect technology in design and use and *vice versa*. This is a constant process because diversities themselves are changing alongside technologies. It is also not an easy process because it could be reasonably presumed that what is beneficial for one group of people might not be beneficial for another. Such complexities need to be reflected on and considered. Different interests and consequences have to be carefully analysed and weighted.

This also requires us to step away from the idea that there are simple fixes that could be applied to technology to ensure that it is inclusive. As I have demonstrated in Chapter 4, algorithmic bias is often seen as something that can be fixed through technical means. There is also a tendency to apply a checkbox mentality to diversity to show that one has considered diversity. Often, such checks only go as far as legally required. However, instead of seeing this form of diversity-proofing as a one-off process, how a specific technology relates to diversity will have to be questioned continuously. It is easy to see how this can lead to 'analysis paralysis' due to the sheer complexity that is entailed in such a process. This is particularly the case once intersectionality is taken into account. While this approach is challenging, it could be a way to ensure that technologies are more inclusive in design and use. We are thus able to design a future that is potentially more inclusive than the past.

Embedding responsibility, accountability and governance in the AI supply chain has, however, proven to be challenging. I have mentioned earlier that it has been suggested that data sets should come with datasheets (Gebru et al., 2021). Others have suggested that data sets should have something similar to nutritional labels (Chmielinski et al., 2022). Such additional detail would include information on how data was collected and processed. However, a key concern with such approaches is the fact that AI supply chains consist of many actors; AI systems are assembled using an array of pre-existing software to which a multitude of people contribute (Widder & Nafus, 2023). Widder and Nafus (2023) critique existing approaches to manage responsibility and accountability as requiring 'panoptical visibility into the technology' (Widder & Nafus, 2023, p. 8), alongside a control over this technology. Widder and Nafus (2023) argue this is rarely the case in the AI supply chain. Since much of the AI supply chain is based on modularity, it has been suggested that accountability should be located within the individual modules (Widder & Nafus, 2023). This echoes the feminist concept of 'located accountabilities' (Suchman, 2002). Additionally, the intersections between modules need to be strengthened, which can include, for instance, that customers check that data labellers are remunerated adequately (Widder & Nafus, 2023). Finally, Widder and Nafus (2023) suggest that modularity might be replaced completely, with a new system such as one based on principles of design justice (Costanza-Chock, 2020).

Another aspect of accountability relates to the fact that we often anthropo-morphise technologies. One meaning of anthropomorphism refers to the process of attributing human characteristics or personality to a non-human entity such as an object or an animal (Oxford English Dictionary, 2023a). For instance, in Chapter 1, we saw how Weizenbaum was bewildered by the fact that people anthropomorphised the chatbot ELIZA (Treusch, 2017). In the books on the future of work that I analysed for this research, a similar tendency to anthropomorphise technologies could also be observed. In Chapter 2, I discussed how Baldwin (2019) describes how customers wanted to date or buy roses for Tiffany, a virtual assistant in a car dealer-ship in Texas. Anthropomorphising is presuming human-like intelligence in machines. Given the fact that AI often is said to emulate human intelligence, this tendency of anthropomorphising is probably not surprising. Although academic research is often critical about anthropomorphising while trying to avoid it, it opens an avenue to think about under what conditions a machine might carry responsibility and accountability. We normally situate accountability and responsibility in those who design new technologies. However, there is possibly scope to reflect on in how far machines could also carry responsibility for certain outcomes. Beyond that, there is also scope to think about accountability and responsibility as shared between various actors. This would then call for developing a more complex understanding of how the social and the technical are mutually constitutive and what this means for accountability and responsibility.

Situating the Research and Future Research Avenues

Finally, I want to reflect on how much the specific period of time during which the research was conducted shaped this book and what future research might explore. As I have outlined in Chapter 1, the research was developed prior to the Covid-19 pandemic and the primary material was collated during different stages of the pandemic, from lockdowns to restrictions being removed. The various levels of restrictions meant that during the time when I would have anticipated doing the bulk of the fieldwork, fieldwork in the traditional sense was not possible. Instead of focusing on a limited set of field sites and a limited set of technologies, I was able to capture experiences and perspectives from people living in various parts of the globe, and I was able to theorise various technologies. For instance, I doubt I would have studied VR without the pandemic limiting face-to-face contact. This allowed me to present a much broader and more encompassing perspective on how digitalisation and gender are intertwined in the future of work.

The pandemic also put specific versions of the future of work to the fore. Questions of how the future of work looks if work is no longer confined to traditional workspaces dominated much of the public discourse. The media is filled with news that employers allow employees to work indefinitely from home, which employees have to return to the office, how office attendance is monitored and so on. This is intertwined with questions about what happens to social interactions if people are not physically in one space. Some employers rushed people back to the physical office as soon as this was possible, pretending that the pandemic and the resulting experimentation with where and how work is conducted does not matter. Others have moved completely virtually, only getting their companies together for special events. In those discussions, it is often forgotten that for many people, the location of work has not changed. Those who pack and deliver online orders and those who provide healthcare did not see their location of work altered much during the pandemic. I have no doubt that the pandemic and the resulting questioning of office as a physical and virtual location will dominate debates in academia and in practice for years to come as a new *status quo* is established.

The time when this research was conducted also coincides with various so-called breakthroughs in regard to technologies. Talking about breakthroughs is in itself problematic because it disguises the social relations that influence the design and development that feed into those presumed breakthroughs. Much of the underlying research and development is incremental. However, what interests me here is how these breakthroughs capture the imagination of people. We might think of Facebook's rebranding as Meta to signal a move into VR (Meta, 2021), Apple's foray into what they call spatial computing (Apple, 2023), and the public launch of Open AI's ChatGPT (OpenAI, 2022). We continue to be amazed and concerned by those developments but they are in themselves just the latest reiteration of the technology *du jour* that is heralded as a 'game changer'. While it would be easy to focus on the latest hype, these technologies are embedded in their specific context. This is also true for the technologies that I explored in this book. However, technologies being contextual does not mean that they do not have wider relevance. As a matter of fact, I advanced the argument throughout this book that the dynamics observed around technologies allow us to see patterns of how technologies are shaping and are shaped by society. Such observations will have purchase beyond the immediate hype.

The question of how digitalisation and gender are intertwined in the workplace and beyond will remain a relevant one. This book has shown a range of patterns that emerge in relation to gender and digitalisation in the work context. Since research is always partial, I am sure that there are a multitude of other patterns that other researchers might be able to trace. For example, exploring how technologies have entered the home to conduct (paid) work during the pandemic will undoubtedly provide a rich backdrop to many studies that explore what it means if kitchen tables at home become a place to work. This of course entailed shifts in relation to unpaid work. While this book has used the definition of work that is dominant in much thinking of the future of work (see Chapter 1), this also opens up the opportunity to think about the future of unpaid work. Although discussions on the future of work tend to centre on paid work, humans spend a lot of time on unpaid domestic work (Lehdonvirta et al., 2023). This changes the debates. We then have to ask '[i]f robots will take our jobs, will they at least also take out the trash for us?' (Lehdonvirta et al., 2023, p. 2). The expectation is that 39% of the time spent on domestic work can be automated within a decade (Lehdonvirta et al., 2023). Yet, what is regarded as automatable differs: physical childcare is perceived as least automatable and shopping for groceries as most automatable (Lehdonvirta et al., 2023). It is interesting to note justifications why childcare is difficult to automate, centred on social factors with delegating childcare to machines being socially not acceptable, alongside concerns for the developmental impact on children and privacy concerns (Lehdonvirta et al., 2023). The points to the fact that not everything that might be technically possible is also socially desirable (see also Chapter 3). Further research illuminating the relationship between gender and digitalisation in debates on the future of work, paid and unpaid, is thus needed.

There is also limited research on workers in the AI supply chain and how their knowledge might or might not be reflected in the data sets that are used for machine learning. How workers often in the Global South and often women label data that is largely used in the Global North for machine learning necessitates further detailed investigations. Further research is also required in regard to the underlying epistemologies and ontologies that are used in machine learning and how they relate to gender, diversity and inclusion. A further area of research would specifically be to explore how intersectionality can be considered in machine learning. Such research would necessarily transcend traditional disciplinary boundaries by combining different disciplinary backgrounds through interdisciplinary research but might well be transdisciplinary (Gibbons et al., 1994; Nowotny, 1999). While this book was able to show dynamic and complex patterns around gender and digitalisation, future research will be able to explore alternative and different ways in which such patterns take shape and matter.

Conclusion

This book has shown how future-shaping patterns around digitalisation and gender emerge are justified and could be changed. In this chapter, I have brought the different threads of these patterns together to show how predicting the future based on data constructs a potential version of the world while making other versions harder to come to pass. I have suggested how seemingly isolated issues taken together form patterns that can foster inclusion or create exclusion. As such, I have argued that the future is socially constructed and that different visions of the future might also lead to constructing different realities. How technologies are shaped, for instance, through data not only means the societal relations are imprinted on data but these technologies also make the unwritten rules – or patterns – of societies visible, allowing an avenue for change. I have also suggested that it is important to consider who shapes these technologies and which perspectives are erased. Overall, the book has developed different threads that, woven together, shed light on how gender and digitalisation are intertwined. It is only by bringing these different threads together that broader patterns emerge.

These patterns speak to complex and dynamic connections between gender and digitalisation that are often overlooked. The book has illustrated how the ideal professional worker is implicitly conceived as a white man who is the breadwinner in the family. We have also seen how certain skills are constructed as uniquely human. We have explored how algorithmic bias in hiring emerges and how the politics of in/visibility are central for data practices. Those patterns point to how exclusion can happen. However, the book has also focused on alternative ways in which technologies can be used to create more inclusion. Technologies such as those that rely on AI are likely to repeat many patterns that have led to exclusion in the past. However, the same shaping effect can also be used to design and use technologies in ways through which patterns emerge that foster inclusion. The book has thus explored in how far these patterns can be changed and altered to allow for more inclusive futures of work. Digitalisation risks repeating traditional patterns of exclusion. However, if technology is understood as shaped by society and *vice versa*, then digitalisation can potentially create new and more inclusive patterns. Since the technologies that are shaped by society today will shape societies in the future, a central task of our time is to ensure that digitalisation means inclusion.

Notes

1 Such care labour is not only gendered but also racialised (Ehrenreich & Hochschild, 2003; Gutiérrez-Rodríguez, 2014).
2 I have made this argument and provided a comic strip for such a scenario in my earlier research (Kelan, 2015).
3 It is difficult to pinpoint this change but I became aware of the fact that many questions in mainstream practitioner-oriented events on gender included audience questions about seeing gender as beyond a binary from about 2014 onwards.
4 Thanks to the authors for allowing me to cite their working paper on that topic.

APPENDIX

Data Collection in Times of a Pandemic and Beyond

The research presented in this book is based on two projects. The first project was funded through a Leverhulme Trust Major Research Fellowship [MRF-2019-069] and is the basis for most of this book. The stated research aim in the proposal was to trace the dynamics of gender and digitalisation in the work context. I proposed to focus on three interrelated research questions. First, how is gender imagined in relation to digitalisation by thought leaders and in popular books on the future of work? Second, how are gender and digitalisation intertwined in professional work? Third, how is gender considered in hiring processes supported by AI? I originally planned to interview experts on the future of work face-to-face and to conduct several fieldwork visits to understand how working practices changed in professional services and how hiring practices change with AI. In addition to this project, I also had funding from a British Academy Small Grant [SRG20\200195]. This grant built on the core idea of the Leverhulme Trust Major research fellowship but focused on a new setting: how data-labelling work that is central to AI is intertwined with gender. I proposed a similar methodological approach for both research projects, consisting of a field visit and interviews (Atkinson, 1990; Hammersley & Atkinson, 1995). Overall, the research was supposed to draw on tried and tested methods, which I had used in various studies before.

I submitted the original proposal for the Leverhulme Trust Major Research Fellowship in early 2019. By the time the research started in the autumn of 2020, the world was in the grip of the Covid-19 pandemic, which required me to change my approach to data collection. The restrictions to work and travel and the change in working patterns meant that I did not conduct fieldwork in the way I had planned. Many of the people I would normally have observed have not returned to the office. Many of the offices have been dissolved. It was challenging to build a rapport with gatekeepers for fieldwork access. Some of the gatekeepers lost their jobs, others stopped responding to my messages. Even when access to field sites was granted, these visits were cancelled due to new Covid-19 restrictions or the business ceasing to operate.

Instead of doing field research in the envisioned form, I relied on interviews that I conducted via online video conferencing. The pandemic normalised speaking to others via Zoom and related technologies. Zoom seems in many ways made for research interviews because it is straightforward to record audio and video. It is also beneficial because one can speak to people in a variety of locations without concerns around travelling there. My sample for the research became more global than I had anticipated.

However, finding people to interview became a major challenge. Rather than interviewing people who worked in one of the field sites, I had to source interviewees through a variety of means. Finding the right type of interviewees was extremely difficult and time-consuming. I mostly relied on identifying individuals and then connecting with them via LinkedIn before approaching them to ask for an interview. I would chase them up to two times. I have sourced, contacted and chased well over 400 people in the course of this research. Recruiting research participants was an extremely slow and rather tedious process.

Once an individual agreed to be interviewed and we agreed a time to talk, it was not uncommon to move the interview multiple times. The ease of moving interviews is an advantage and drawback of online interviewing – if I would be sitting in reception waiting to be picked up for an interview, it is less likely that an interview does not take place. For this research, I was often waiting in the Zoom call to be told that we had to move the meeting. Given that most of the individuals are busy professionals, that is not surprising. In some cases, the cancelled interviews were not rescheduled, which I understood as people not wanting to participate in the research anymore.

Another difference to interviews I conducted before is that snowballing – asking research participants to suggest others I can speak to – did not really work. Often, individuals would mention that they would ask colleagues, but even after reminding them, it was rare that this was successful. I regularly followed up with names I had been given but even that did not work. In relation to the data-labelling work, the field was so small that many of the interviewees suggested one another. One notable exception when snowballing worked well was a HR consultant who introduced me to a hiring technology company who in turn facilitated contact to a whole range of interviewees. Overall, finding interviewees and interviewing them took much more time than with any other project I had done before.

I conducted different waves of interviews over the course of the research. The interviews with the experts on the future of work started in 2021. In 2022, I then began interviewing in relation to hiring, professional work and data labelling. Those interviews continued up to early 2024. I was thus able to capture various ways in which the pandemic influenced working life, but also how the talk about technologies changed over time.

The names of the people I interviewed for this research and that are referenced in this book are not their real names but pseudonyms. Overall, I conducted 73 interviews. Sixty-nine were formal interviews. The interviews lasted an hour and were recorded. I asked interviewees to indicate their preferred pronouns when I formally interviewed them. Thirty-six used the pronoun he/him, 30 interviewees used she/her, 2 they/them and 1 she/they. The majority of interviewees were based in the UK, followed by those based in the United States and Europe. A couple of interviewees were based in Australia and one in the United Arab Emirates. The majority of those interviewed indicated that they identified as white, with a few indicating that they were South Asian, Latin American, Asian or mixed backgrounds including Black and African. In terms of age, the largest group of interviewees indicated to be born in the 1980s, followed by those born in the 1990s, 1970s and 1960s, with one interviewee indicating being born in the 1950s. In addition, I conducted four informal interviews, which were not recorded but where I took notes that informed the research. Most interviews were conducted in English, with some being conducted in German.

The pandemic also meant that I explored other methods of collecting data, such as immersing myself into VR. This was akin to auto-ethnography

(Hibbert et al., 2022; Hine, 2020). The downside of this form of material collection is that observation provides richer material on how work gets done. When I job-shadow individuals, I would normally be participating in most of their daily activities and I would be able to join meetings. This became more complex during a pandemic, when shadowing a person working from home seemed strange and most people felt uncomfortable for me to participate in virtual meetings. I also missed all the water cooler and corridor talk that is normally very informative for research.

While much of the research was affected by the pandemic, analysing the books on the future of work meant that I was able to capture discussions on the future of work pre-pandemic. Only a few books make reference to Covid-19, which is due to the fact that the cut-off time for inclusion was 2020, and even those books published in 2020 included only marginal references to Covid-19. This is unsurprising given the fact that most of the books were in production when the pandemic started. Through the interviews, I then traced the different phases of the pandemic, with its global variations ending in a time period where the struggle for the new *status quo* when and where work is done is still continuing.

When analysing the books on the future of work, I read each book twice and copied relevant sections into a document. The interviews were recorded via Zoom and a back-up recording and then transcribed by a professional transcription service. I proofread each transcript. When I used technologies myself, I drew on what has been called the technology walkthrough method (Ritter, 2022; Light et al., 2018); for instance, recording myself in Zoom while using the Oculus Quest 2 and having Zoom create a transcript. Although the transcript was of mixed quality, together with the video recorded, it allowed me to analyse the material in depth. I also took field notes on my experiences. The transcripts (notes from books, interviews, technology walkthrough, field notes) were imported into NVivo, a qualitative research software, and then coded. The codes provided the basis for my analysis presented in this book.

Without the Covid-19 pandemic, the research would have undoubtedly looked very different. The pandemic has influenced how the material was collected but also permeated many of the interviews. The project itself changed significantly with the pandemic in terms of how I collected the data. However, the project did not change in regard to what I was interested in researching.

REFERENCES

Abdullah, M., Madain, A., & Jararweh, Y. (2022). ChatGPT: Fundamentals, applications and social impacts. In P. Ceravolo, C. Guetl, Y. Jararweh, & E. BenKhelifa (Eds.), *Proceedings of the Ninth International Conference on Social Networks Analysis, Management and Security (SNAMS)* (pp. 223–229). New York: IEEE.

Acker, J. (1990). Hierarchies, jobs, bodies: A theory of gendered organizations. *Gender & Society, 4*(2), 139–158.

Acker, J. (2006). Inequality regimes: Gender, class, and race in organizations. *Gender & Society, 20*(4), 441–464.

Adam, A. (1998). *Artificial Knowing: Gender and the Thinking Machine*. New York: Routledge.

Aguinis, H., Villamor, I., & Ramani, R. S. (2021). MTurk research: Review and recommendations. *Journal of Management, 47*(4), 823–837.

Albert, E. T. (2019). AI in talent acquisition: A review of AI-applications used in recruitment and selection. *Strategic HR Review, 18*(5), 215–221.

Amankwah-Amoah, J., Khan, Z., Wood, G., & Knight, G. (2021). COVID-19 and digitalization: The great acceleration. *Journal of Business Research, 136*, 602–611.

Anti-Diskriminierungsstelle des Bundes (2023). *Frau – Mann – Divers: Die "Dritte Option" und das Allgemeine Gleichbehandlungsgesetz (AGG)*. Retrieved from https://rb.gy/677qpg

Apple (2023). Introducing Apple Vision Pro: Apple's first spatial computer. *Apple Newsroom*, 5 June. Retrieved from www.apple.com/uk/newsroom/2023/06/introducing-apple-vision-pro/

Atkinson, P. (1990). *The Ethnographic Imagination: Textual Constructions of Reality*. London: Routledge.

Autor, D., Mindell, D., & Reynolds, E. (2023). *The Work of the Future: Building Better Jobs in an Age of Intelligent Machines*. Cambridge, MA: MIT Press.

Autor, D. H. (2015). Why are there still so many jobs? The history and future of workplace automation. *Journal of Economic Perspectives*, 29(3), 3–30.

Baldwin, R. (2019). *The Globotics Upheaval: Globalization, Robotics and the Future of Work*. Oxford: Oxford University Press.

Balliester, T., & Elsheikhi, A. (2018). *The Future of Work: A Literature Review*. ILO Research Department Working Paper No. 29, International Labour Office, Geneva.

Baraniuk, C. (2022, 14 June). From reinforcing entrenched gender roles to potentially even fuelling misogyny, choosing the right voice for a particular task can be a minefield. *BBC*, Retrieved 9 February 2024, www.bbc.com/future/article/20220614-why-your-voice-assistant-might-be-sexist

Barocas, S., & Selbst, A. D. (2016). Big data's disparate impact. *California Law Review*, 104, 671–732.

BBC News (2018, 10 October). Amazon scrapped "sexist AI" tool. *BBC News*. Retrieved from www.bbc.co.uk/news/technology-45809919

Bechmann, A., & Bowker, G. C. (2019). Unsupervised by any other name: Hidden layers of knowledge production in artificial intelligence on social media. *Big Data & Society*, 6(1). https://doi.org/10.1177/2053951718819569

Benanav, A. (2020). *Automation and the Future of Work*. London: Verso.

Benjamin, R. (2019). *Race After Technology: Abolitionist Tools for the New Jim Code*. Cambridge: Polity.

Bessen, J. (2015). Toil and technology: Innovative technology is displacing workers to new jobs rather than replacing them entirely. *Finance & Development*, 52(1), 16–19.

Biddle Consulting Group (2023). Uniform guidelines on employee selection procedures. Retrieved from www.uniformguidelines.com

Black, J. S., & Van Esch, P. (2020). AI-enabled recruiting: What is it and how should a manager use it? *Business Horizons*, 63(2), 215–226.

Black, S. L., Stone, D. L., & Johnson, A. F. (2015). Use of social networking websites on applicants' privacy. *Employee Responsibilities and Rights Journal*, 27(2), 115–159.

Bowker, G. C., & Star, S. L. (2000). *Sorting Things Out*. Cambridge, MA: MIT Press.

Broussard, M. (2018). *Artificial Unintelligence: How Computers Misunderstand the World*. Cambridge, MA: MIT Press.

Bui, L. (2020). Asian roboticism: Connecting mechanized labor to the automation of work. *Perspectives on Global Development and Technology*, 19(1–2), 110–126.

Buolamwini, J., & Gebru, T. (2018). Gender shades: Intersectional accuracy disparities in commercial gender classification. In *Proceedings of Machine Learning Research Vol. 81: Conference on Fairness, Accountability and*

Transparency, 23–24 February 2018, New York (pp. 77–91). Maastricht: ML Research Press.

Buolamwini, J., Gebru, T., Raynham, H., Raji, D., & Zuckerman, E. (2023). Gender shades. *Gender Shades* [website], n.d. Retrieved from http://gende rshades.org/overview.html

Buranyi, S. (2018, 4 March). How to persuade a robot that you should get the job. *The Observer.* Retrieved from www.theguardian.com/technology/2018/mar/04/robots-screen-candidates-for-jobs-artificial-intelligence

Bursell, M., & Roumbanis, L. (2024). After the algorithms: A study of meta-algorithmic judgments and diversity in the hiring process at a large multi-site company. *Big Data & Society, 11*(1), 1–18.

Butler, J. (1990). *Gender Trouble: Feminism and the Subversion of Identity.* London: Routledge.

Caliskan, A., Bryson, J. J., & Narayanan, A. (2017). Semantics derived automatically from language corpora contain human-like biases. *Science, 356*(6334), 183–186.

Čapek, K. (1920). *R.U.R.: Rossum's Universal Robots.* Cabin John, MD: Wildside Press.

Carli, L. L. (2020). Women, gender equality and COVID-19. *Gender in Management: An International Journal, 35*(7/8), 647–655.

Cave, S. (2020). The problem with intelligence: Its value-laden history and the future of AI. In *AIES '20: Proceedings of the AAAI/ACM Conference on AI, Ethics, and Society* (pp. 29–35). New York: ACM.

Chalmers, D. J. (2022). *Reality+: Virtual Worlds and the Problems of Philosophy.* London: Allen Lane.

Cheng, M. M., & Hackett, R. D. (2021). A critical review of algorithms in HRM: Definition, theory, and practice. *Human Resource Management Review, 31*(1), art. 100698.

Chevallier, M. (2023). Staging Paro: The care of making robot(s) care. *Social Studies of Science, 53*(5), 635–659.

Chmielinski, K. S., Newman, S., Taylor, M., Joseph, J., Thomas, K., Yurkofsky, J., & Qiu, Y. C. (2022). The dataset nutrition label (2nd gen): Leveraging context to mitigate harms in artificial intelligence. Paper presented at NeurIPS 2020 Workshop on Dataset Curation and Security. Retrieved from https://arxiv.org/abs/2201.03954

Cockburn, C., & Ormrod, S. (1993). *Gender & Technology in the Making.* London: Sage.

Costanza-Chock, S. (2020). *Design Justice: Community-Led Practices to Build the Worlds We Need.* Cambridge, MA: MIT Press.

Cowan, R. S. (1983). *More Work for Mother: The Ironies of Household Technology from the Open Hearth to the Microwave.* New York: Basic Books.

Cowan, R. S. (1999). How the refrigerator got its hum. In D. MacKenzie, & J. Wajcman (Eds.), *The Social Shaping of Technology* (pp. 202–218). Milton Keynes: Open University Press.

Crawford, K. (2021). *The Atlas of AI*. New Haven, CT: Yale University Press.

Crenshaw, K. W. (1989). Demarginalizing the intersection of race and sex: A black feminist critique of antidiscrimination doctrine, feminist theory, and antiracist politics. *University of Chicago Legal Forum, 14*, 538–554.

D'Ignazio, C., & Klein, L. F. (2020). *Data Feminism*. Cambridge, MA: MIT Press.

Dalenberg, D. J. (2018). Preventing discrimination in the automated targeting of job advertisements. *Computer Law & Security Review, 34*(3), 615–627.

Danaher, J. (2022). Techno-optimism: An analysis, an evaluation and a modest defence. *Philosophy & Technology, 35*(2), art. 54.

Dastin, J. (2018, 11 October). Amazon scraps secret AI recruiting tool that showed bias against women. *Reuters*. Retrieved from www.reuters.com/arti cle/us-amazon-com-jobs-automation-insight/amazon-scraps-secret-ai-rec ruiting-tool-that-showed-bias-against-women-idUSKCN1MK08G

Datta, A., Tschantz, M. C., & Datta, A. (2014). Automated experiments on ad privacy settings: A tale of opacity, choice, and discrimination. *Proceedings on Privacy Enhancing Technologies, 2015*(1), 92–112.

Daugherty, P. R., & Wilson, H. J. (2018). *Human + Machine: Reimagining Work in the Age of AI*. Boston, MA: Harvard Business Press.

Davani, A. M., Díaz, M., & Prabhakaran, V. (2022). Dealing with disagreements: Looking beyond the majority vote in subjective annotations. *Transactions of the Association for Computational Linguistics, 10*, 92–110.

De Cremer, D. (2020). *Leadership by Algorithm: Who Leads and Who Follows in the AI Era?* Petersfield: Harriman House.

De Smet, A., Dowling, B., Mugayar-Baldocchi, M., & Schaninger, B. (2021). "Great Attrition" or "Great Attraction"? The choice is yours. *McKinsey Quarterly*, 8 September. Retrieved from www.mckinsey.com/business-functi ons/people-and-organizational-performance/our-insights/great-attrition-or-great-attraction-the-choice-is-yours

Denton, E., Hanna, A., Amironesei, R., Smart, A., Nicole, H., & Scheuerman, M. K. (2020). *Bringing the people back in: Contesting benchmark machine learning datasets*. Research paper. Retrieved from https://arxiv.org/pdf/2007.07399

Devlin, K., & Belton, O. (2020). The measure of a woman: Fembots, fact and fiction. In S. Cave, K. Dihal, & S. Dillon (Eds.), *AI Narratives* (pp. 357–381). Oxford: Oxford University Press.

Dillon, S. (2020). The Eliza effect and its dangers: From demystification to gender critique. *Journal for Cultural Research, 24*(1), 1–15.

Domingos, P. (2015). *The Master Algorithm: How the Quest for the Ultimate Learning Machine Will Remake Our World*. London: Penguin.

Drage, E., & Frabetti, F. (2023). AI that matters: A feminist approach to the study of intelligent machines. In J. Browne, S. Cave, E. Drage, & K. McInerney

(Eds.), *Feminist AI: Critical Perspectives on Algorithms, Data, and Intelligent Machines* (pp. 274–290). Oxford: Oxford University Press.

Duden (2023). Türken. *Duden* [online dictionary]. Retrieved from www.duden.de/rechtschreibung/tuerken

Dwork, C., Hardt, M., Pitassi, T., Reingold, O., & Zemel, R. (2012). Fairness through awareness. In *Proceedings of the 3rd Innovations in Theoretical Computer Science Conference* (pp. 214–226). New York: ACM.

Edwards, M., & Edwards, K. (2019). *Predictive HR Analytics: Mastering the HR Metric*. London: Kogan Page.

Ehrenreich, B., & Hochschild, A. R. (2003). *Global Woman: Nannies, Maids, and Sex Workers in the New Economy*. New York: Metropolitan.

Eldan, R., & Li, Y. (2023). *TinyStories: How small can language models be and still speak coherent English?* Research paper. Retrieved from https://arxiv.org/pdf/2305.07759

Ely, R. (1995). The power in demography: Women's social constructions of gender identity at work. *Academy of Management Journal, 38*(3), 589–634.

England, K., & Lawson, V. (2005). Feminist analyses of work: Rethinking the boundaries, gendering, and spatiality of work. In L. Nelson, & J. Seager (Eds.), *A Companion to Feminist Geography* (pp. 77–92). Oxford: Blackwell.

Equals & UNESCO (2019). I'd blush if I could: Closing gender divides in digital skills through education. Retrieved 13 December 2020, http://repositorio.minedu.gob.pe/handle/MINEDU/6598

Eubanks, B. (2018). *Artificial Intelligence for HR: Use AI to Support and Develop a Successful Workforce*. London: Kogan Page.

Eubanks, V. (2018). *Automating Inequality: How High-Tech Tools Profile, Police, and Punish the Poor*. New York: St. Martin's Press.

European Parliament (2024). *Artificial Intelligence Act*. www.europarl.europa.eu/doceo/document/TA-9-2024-0138-FNL-COR01_EN.pdf

Faulkner, W. (2001). The technology question in feminism: A view from feminist technology studies. *Women's Studies International Forum, 24*(1), 79–95.

Fausto-Sterling, A. (2000). *Sexing the Body: Gender Politics and the Construction of Sexuality*. New York: Basic Books.

Feloni, R. (2017, 28 June). Consumer-goods giant Unilever has been hiring employees using brain games and artificial intelligence – and it's a huge success. *Business Insider*. Retrieved from www.businessinsider.com/unilever-artificial-intelligence-hiring-process-2017-6

Finn, E. (2017). *What Algorithms Want: Imagination in the Age of Computing*. Cambridge, MA: MIT Press.

Fisher, A. N., & Ryan, M. K. (2021). Gender inequalities during COVID-19. *Group Processes & Intergroup Relations, 24*(2), 237–245.

Fletcher, J. K. (1999). *Disappearing Acts: Gender, Power, and Relational Practice at Work*. Cambridge, MA: MIT Press.

Fletcher, J. K. (2004). The paradox of postheroic leadership: An essay on gender, power, and transformational change. *The Leadership Quarterly*, 15(5), 647–661.

Flor, L. S., Friedman, J., Spencer, C. N., Cagney, J., Arrieta, A., Herbert, M. E., Stein, C., Mullany, E. C., Hon, J., & Patwardhan, V. (2022). Quantifying the effects of the COVID-19 pandemic on gender equality on health, social, and economic indicators: A comprehensive review of data from March, 2020, to September, 2021. *The Lancet*, 399(10344), 2381–2397.

Frey, C. B. (2019). *The Technology Trap: Capital, Labor, and Power in the Age of Automation*. Princeton, NJ: Princeton University Press.

Frey, C. B., & Osborne, M. A. (2017). The future of employment: How susceptible are jobs to computerisation? *Technological Forecasting and Social Change*, 114, 254–280.

Garfinkel, H. (1984). Passing and the managed achievement of sex status in an "intersexed" person. In H. Garfinkel, *Studies in Ethnomethodology* (pp. 116–186). Cambridge: Polity Press.

Gebru, T., Morgenstern, J., Vecchione, B., Vaughan, J. W., Wallach, H., Daumé, H., III, & Crawford, K. (2021). *Datasheets for datasets*. Research Paper. Retrieved from https://arxiv.org/pdf/1803.09010.pdf

GenderLess Voice (2023). Meet Q. *GenderLess Voice* [website]. Retrieved from www.genderlessvoice.com/

Genova, J. (1994). Turing's sexual guessing game. *Social Epistemology*, 8(4), 313–326.

Geoghegan, B. D. (2020). Orientalism and informatics: Alterity from the chess-playing Turk to Amazon's Mechanical Turk. *Ex-position*, 43, 45–90.

Gibbons, M., Limoges, C., Nowotny, H., Schwartzman, S., Scott, P., & Trow, M. (1994). *The New Production of Knowledge: The Dynamics of Science and Research in Contemporary Societies*. London: Sage.

Gill, R., & Orgad, S. (2022). Get unstuck! Pandemic positivity imperatives and self-care for women. *Cultural Politics*, 18(1), 44–63.

Goffman, E. (1979). *Gender Advertisements*. London: Macmillan.

Gray, M. L., & Suri, S. (2019). *Ghost Work: How to Stop Silicon Valley from Building a New Global Underclass*. New York: Houghton Mifflin Harcourt.

Grosman, J., & Reigeluth, T. (2019). Perspectives on algorithmic normativities: Engineers, objects, activities. *Big Data & Society*, 6(2). https://doi.org/10.1177/2053951719858742

Gunasekar, S., Zhang, Y., Aneja, J., Mendes, C. C. T., Del Giorno, A., Gopi, S., Javaheripi, M., Kauffmann, P., De Rosa, G., & Saarikivi, O. (2023). *Textbooks are all you need*. Research paper. Retrieved from https://arxiv.org/pdf/2306.11644

Gutiérrez-Rodríguez, E. (2014). The precarity of feminisation. *International Journal of Politics, Culture, and Society*, 27(2), 191–202.

Hammersley, M., & Atkinson, P. (1995). *Ethnography: Principles in Practice* (2nd ed.). London: Routledge.

Haraway, D. (1991). Situated knowledges: The science question in feminism and the privilege of partial perspective. In D. Haraway (Ed.), *Simians, Cyborgs and Women: The Reinvention of Nature* (pp. 183–201). London: Free Association.

Harlan, E., & Schnuck, O. (2023). Objective or biased: On the questionable use of AI in job applications. *Bayerischer Rundfunk* [website], n.d. Retrieved from https://web.br.de/interaktiv/ki-bewerbung/en/

Hatzius, J., Briggs, J., Kodnani, D., & Pierdomenico, G. (2023, 26 March). The potentially large effects of artificial intelligence on economic growth. *Goldman Sachs* [website]. Retrieved from www.gspublishing.com/content/research/en/reports/2023/03/27/d64e052b-0f6e-45d7-967b-d7be35fabd16.html

Hawksworth, J., Berriman, R., & Goel, S. (2018). *Will Robots Really Steal Our Jobs? An International Analysis of the Potential Long Term Impact of Automation.* London: PwC. Retrieved from www.pwc.co.uk/economic-services/assets/international-impact-of-automation-feb-2018.pdf

Hayes, P., & Ford, K. (1995). Turing test considered harmful. In *IJCAI '95: Proceedings of the 14th International Joint Conference on Artificial Intelligence* (pp. 972–977). San Francisco, CA: Morgan Kaufmann.

Henriksen, A., & Bechmann, A. (2020). Building truths in AI: Making predictive algorithms doable in healthcare. *Information, Communication & Society*, 23(6), 802–816.

Hibbert, P., Beech, N., Callagher, L., & Siedlok, F. (2022). After the pain: Reflexive practice, emotion work and learning. *Organization Studies*, 43(5), 797–817.

Hicks, M. (2018). *Programmed Inequality*. Cambridge, MA: MIT Press.

Hine, C. (2020). Strategies for reflexive ethnography in the smart home: Autoethnography of silence and emotion. *Sociology*, 54(1), 22–36.

Hofmann, J. (1999). Writers, texts and writing acts: Gendered user images in word processing software. In D. MacKenzie, & J. Wajcman (Eds.), *The Social Shaping of Technology* (pp. 222–243). Milton Keynes: Open University Press.

Hoffman, M., Kahn, L. B., & Li, D. (2015). *Discretion in Hiring*. NBER Working Paper No. 21709. Retrieved from www.nber.org/papers/w21709

Hofstadter, D. R. (1995). *Fluid Concepts and Creative Analogies: Computer Models of the Fundamental Mechanisms of Thought.* New York: BasicBooks.

Howcroft, D., & Bergvall-Kåreborn, B. (2019). A typology of crowdwork platforms. *Work, Employment and Society*, 33(1), 21–38.

Howcroft, D., & Rubery, J. (2019). "Bias in, bias out": Gender equality and the future of work debate. *Labour & Industry*, 29(2), 213–227.

Howcroft, D., & Taylor, P. (2023). Automation and the future of work: A social shaping of technology approach. *New Technology, Work and Employment*, 38(2), 351–370.

Imana, B., Korolova, A., & Heidemann, J. (2021). Auditing for discrimination in algorithms delivering job ads. In J. Lescovec, M. Grobelnik, M. Najork, J. Tang, & L. Zia (Eds.), *WWW '21: Proceedings of the Web Conference* (pp. 3767–3778). New York: ACM.

Irani, L. (2015). The cultural work of microwork. *New Media & Society, 17*(5), 720–739.

Irani, L. (2016). The hidden faces of automation. *Crossroads: The ACM Magazine for Students, 23*(2), 34–37.

Jacobsen, B. N. (2023). Machine learning and the politics of synthetic data. *Big Data & Society, 10*(1). doi.org/10.1177/20539517221145372

Jasanoff, S. (2015). Future imperfect: Science, technology, and the imaginations of modernity. In S. Jasanoff, & S.-H. Kim (Eds.), *Dreamscapes of Modernity: Sociotechnical Imaginaries and the Fabrication of Power* (pp. 1–33). Chicago, IL: University of Chicago Press.

Jaton, F. (2017). We get the algorithms of our ground truths: Designing referential databases in digital image processing. *Social Studies of Science, 47*(6), 811–840.

Jaton, F. (2021). *The Constitution of Algorithms: Ground-Truthing, Programming, Formulating.* Cambridge, MA: MIT Press.

Jeske, D., Lippke, S., & Shultz, K. S. (2019). Predicting self-disclosure in recruitment in the context of social media screening. *Employee Responsibilities and Rights Journal, 31*, 99–112.

Johnson, R. D., Stone, D. L., & Lukaszewski, K. M. (2021). The benefits of eHRM and AI for talent acquisition. *Journal of Tourism Futures, 7*(1), 40–52.

Kang, E. B. (2023). Ground truth tracings (GTT): On the epistemic limits of machine learning. *Big Data & Society, 10*(1). https://doi.org/10.1177/205395 17221146122

Kearns, M., & Roth, A. (2019). *The Ethical Algorithm: The Science of Socially Aware Algorithm Design.* Oxford: Oxford University Press.

Kelan, E. (2023a). *Men Stepping Forward: Leading Your Organization on the Path to Inclusion.* Bristol: Bristol University Press.

Kelan, E. K. (2007). Tools and toys: Communicating gendered positions towards technology. *Information, Communication & Society, 10*(3), 357–382.

Kelan, E. K. (2008a). Emotions in a rational profession: The gendering of skills in ICT work. *Gender, Work & Organization, 15*(1), 49–71.

Kelan, E. K. (2008b). The discursive construction of gender in contemporary management literature. *Journal of Business Ethics, 18*(2), 427–445.

Kelan, E. K. (2009). *Performing Gender at Work.* Basingstoke: Palgrave.

Kelan, E. K. (2010). Gender logic and (un)doing gender at work. *Gender, Work & Organization, 17*(2), 174–194.

Kelan, E. K. (2015). *Linchpin: Men, Middle Managers and Gender Inclusive Leadership.* Bedford: Cranfield University.

Kelan, E. K. (2023b). Automation anxiety and augmentation aspiration: Subtexts of the future of work. *British Journal of Management, 34*(4), 2057–2074.

Kelan, E. K. (2024). Algorithmic inclusion: Shaping the predictive algorithms of artificial intelligence in hiring. *Human Resource Management Journal*, early view, https://doi.org/10.1111/1748-8583.12511

Kelan, E. K., & Wratil, P. (2021). CEOs as agents of change and continuity. *Equality, Diversity and Inclusion: An International Journal, 40*(5), 493–509.

Keyes, O. (2018). The misgendering machines: Trans/HCI implications of automatic gender recognition. In Karahalios, K., Monroy-Hernández, A., Lampinen, A., & Fitzpatrick, G. (Eds.), *Proceedings of the ACM on Human-Computer Interaction*, Vol. 2 (art. 88). New York: ACM.

Knight, W. (2021, 12 January). Facial analysis. *Wired*. Retrieved from www.wired.com/story/job-screening-service-halts-facial-analysis-applicants/

Köchling, A., & Wehner, M. C. (2020). Discriminated by an algorithm: A systematic review of discrimination and fairness by algorithmic decision-making in the context of HR recruitment and HR development. *Business Research, 13*(3), 795–848.

Kokot-Blamey, P. (2021). Mothering in accounting: Feminism, motherhood, and making partnership in accountancy in Germany and the UK. *Accounting, Organizations and Society, 93*, art. 101255.

Kokot-Blamey, P. (2023). *Gendered Hierarchies of Dependency: Women Making Partnership in Accountancy Firms*. Oxford: Oxford University Press.

Königs, P. (2022). What is techno-optimism? *Philosophy & Technology, 35*(3), art. 63.

Kuhar, R., & Paternotte, D. (2017). *Anti-Gender Campaigns in Europe: Mobilizing Against Equality*. Lanham, MD: Rowman & Littlefield.

Lee, N. T., Resnick, P., & Barton, G. (2019, 22 May). Algorithmic bias detection and mitigation: Best practices and policies to reduce consumer harms. *Brookings*. Retrieved from www.brookings.edu/research/algorithmic-bias-detection-and-mitigation-best-practices-and-policies-to-reduce-consumer-harms/

Lee, T. B. (2023, 8 December). The real research behind the wild rumors about OpenAI's Q* project. *Ars Technica*. Retrieved from https://arstechnica.com/ai/2023/12/the-real-research-behind-the-wild-rumors-about-openais-q-project/

Lehdonvirta, V., Shi, L. P., Hertog, E., Nagase, N., & Ohta, Y. (2023). The future(s) of unpaid work: How susceptible do experts from different backgrounds think the domestic sphere is to automation? *PLOS ONE, 18*(2), https://doi.org/10.1371/journal.pone.0281282

Light, B., Burgess, J., & Duguay, S. (2018). The walkthrough method: An approach to the study of apps. *New Media & Society, 20*(3), 881–900.

Lum, K., & Chowdhury, R. (2021, 26 February). What is an "algorithm"? It depends whom you ask. *MIT Technology Review*. Retrieved from www.techn ologyreview.com/2021/02/26/1020007/what-is-an-algorithm/

Lupu, I. (2012). Approved routes and alternative paths: The construction of women's careers in large accounting firms – Evidence from the French Big Four. *Critical Perspectives on Accounting, 23*(4–5), 351–369.

MacKenzie, D., & Wajcman, J. (1999). *The Social Shaping of Technology*. Milton Keynes: Open University Press.

MacKenzie, D. A., & Wajcman, J. (1985). *The Social Shaping of Technology: How the Refrigerator Got Its Hum*. Milton Keynes: Open University Press.

Mahalingam, R., & Selvaraj, P. (2023). Caste, epistemic erasure, dignity, and the reproduction of inequalities. Unpublished paper.

Mahardi, Wang, I.-H., Lee, K. C., & Chang, S. L. (2020). Images classification of dogs and cats using fine-tuned VGG models. In T.-H. Meen (Ed.), *Proceedings of the IEEE Eurasia Conference on IOT, Communication and Engineering* (pp. 230–233). New York: IEEE.

Manyika, J., Chui, M., & Miremadi, M. (2017). *A Future that Works: AI, Automation, Employment, and Productivity*. New York: McKinsey Global Institute.

Manyika, J., Lund, S., Chui, M., Bughin, J., Woetzel, J., Batra, P., Ko, R., & Sanghvi, S. (2017). *Jobs Lost, Jobs Gained: Workforce Transitions in a Time of Automation*. New York: McKinsey Global Institute.

Mavin, S., & Yusupova, M. (2020). Gendered experiences of leading and managing through COVID-19: Patriarchy and precarity. *Gender in Management: An International Journal, 35*(7/8), 737–744.

McAfee, A., & Brynjolfsson, E. (2014). *The Second Machine Age: Work, Progress, and Prosperity in a Time of Brilliant Technologies*. New York: WW Norton.

McAfee, A., & Brynjolfsson, E. (2017). *Machine, Platform, Crowd: Harnessing Our Digital Future*. New York: WW Norton & Company.

McCall, L. (2005). The complexity of intersectionality. *Signs, 30*, 1771–1800.

McCluskey, R., Enshaei, A., & Hasan, B. A. S. (2021). *Finding the Ground-Truth from Multiple Labellers: Why Parameters of the Task Matter*. Working paper, Newcastle University. Retrieved from https://arxiv.org/abs/2102.08482

McIlvaine, A. R. (2018, 5 June). Data in the driver's seat. *Human Resource Executive*. Retrieved from https://hrexecutive.com/talent-acquisitions-lead ers-use-ai-to-improve-hiring/

McKinsey (2020). How COVID-19 has pushed companies over the technology tipping point – and transformed business forever. *McKinsey & Company* [website], 5 October. Retrieved from www.mckinsey.com/capabilities/strat egy-and-corporate-finance/our-insights/how-covid-19-has-pushed-compan ies-over-the-technology-tipping-point-and-transformed-business-forever#/

Merisotis, J. (2020). *Human Work in the Age of Smart Machines*. New York: RosettaBooks.

Meta (2021, 28 October). Introducing Meta: A social technology company. *Meta* [website]. Retrieved from https://about.fb.com/news/2021/10/faceb ook-company-is-now-meta/

Miceli, M., Schuessler, M., & Yang, T. (2020). Between subjectivity and impos- ition. In J. Nichols (Ed.), *Proceedings of the ACM on Human-Computer Interaction*, Vol. 4 (art. 115). New York: ACM.

Miceli, M., Yang, T., Naudts, L., Schuessler, M., Serbanescu, D., & Hanna, A. (2021). Documenting computer vision datasets. In *Proceedings of the 2021 ACM Conference on Fairness, Accountability, and Transparency* (pp. 161–172). New York: ACM.

Mohanty, C. T. (1986). Under Western eyes: Feminist scholarship and post- colonial discourses. *Boundary 2, 12*(3), 333–358.

Mollick, E. (2022, 14 December). ChatGPT is a tipping point for AI. *Harvard Business Review*. Retrieved from https://hbr.org/2022/12/chatgpt-is-a-tipp ing-point-for-ai

Mondragon, N. (2018, 26 March). What is adverse impact? And why meas- uring it matters. *HireVue*. Retrieved from www.hirevue.com/blog/hiring/ what-is-adverse-impact-and-why-measuring-it-matters

Murgia, M. (2019, 24 July). AI's new workforce: The data-labelling industry spreads globally. *Financial Times*. Retrieved from www.ft.com/content/56dde 36c-aa40-11e9-984c-fac8325aaa04

Nash, J. C. (2008). Re-thinking intersectionality. *Feminist Review, 89*(1), 1–15.

Natale, S. (2019). If software is narrative: Joseph Weizenbaum, artificial intel- ligence and the biographies of ELIZA. *New Media & Society, 21*(3), 712–728.

Nentwich, J. C., & Kelan, E. K. (2014). Towards a topology of "doing gender": An analysis of empirical research and its challenges. *Gender, Work & Organization, 21*(2), 121–134.

Noble, S. U. (2018). *Algorithms of Oppression: How Search Engines Reinforce Racism*. New York: New York University Press.

Nowotny, H. (1999). *Es Ist So: Es Könnte Auch Anders Sein*. Frankfurt: Suhrkamp.

Nowotny, H. (2021). *In AI We Trust: Power, Illusion and Control of Predictive Algorithms*. Cambridge: Polity.

O'Connor, S. (2023, 30 May). Don't bet against the "suitcase principle" of white-collar work. *Financial Times*. Retrieved from www.ft.com/content/125fa 211-b973-4cef-aa77-9c8cbc734687

O'Neil, C. (2016). *Weapons of Math Destruction*. London: Penguin.

Oakley, A. (2018). *The Sociology of Housework*. Bristol: Policy Press.

OECD (2016). *Policy Brief on the Future of Work: Automation and Independent Work in a Digital Economy*. Paris: OECD.

OECD (2019). *Recommendation of the Council on Artificial Intelligence*. Paris: OECD. Retrieved from https://legalinstruments.oecd.org/en/inst ruments/OECD-LEGAL-0449

OpenAI (2022, 30 November). Introducing ChatGPT. *OpenAI Blog*. Retrieved from https://openai.com/blog/chatgpt

Oxford English Dictionary (2023a). Anthropomorphism, n., sense 1.b. *OED Online*. Retrieved from https://doi.org/10.1093/OED/9437934606

Oxford English Dictionary (2023b). Automation, n. *OED Online*. Retrieved from https://doi.org/10.1093/OED/8924505997

Oxford English Dictionary (2023c). Digitalization. *OED Online*. Retrieved from https://doi.org/10.1093/OED/7375238048

Oxford English Dictionary (2023d). Digitization. *OED Online*. Retrieved from https://doi.org/10.1093/OED/8455504245

Oxford English Dictionary (2023e). Robot. *OED Online*. Retrieved from https://doi.org/10.1093/OED/5766347792

PARO (2023). PARO therapeutic robot. *PARO* [website]. Retrieved from www.parorobots.com

Pasquale, F. (2015). *The Black Box Society*. Cambridge, MA: Harvard University Press.

Paullada, A., Raji, I. D., Bender, E. M., Denton, E., & Hanna, A. (2021). Data and its (dis)contents: A survey of dataset development and use in machine learning research. *Patterns*, 2(11), art. 100336.

Perrigo, B. (2022, 14 February). Inside Facebook's African sweatshop. *Time*. Retrieved from https://time.com/6147458/facebook-africa-content-moderation-employee-treatment/

Perrigo, B. (2023, 18 January). OpenAI used Kenyan workers on less than $2 per hour to make ChatGPT less toxic. *Time*. Retrieved from https://time.com/6247678/openai-chatgpt-kenya-workers/

Pilling, D. (2024, 11 January). The young people sifting through the internet's worst horrors. *Financial Times*. Retrieved from www.ft.com/content/ef42e78f-e578-450b-9e43-36fbd1e20d01

Pilling, D., & Murgia, M. (2023, 18 May). "You can't unsee it": The content moderators taking on Facebook. *Financial Times*. Retrieved from www.ft.com/content/afeb56f2-9ba5-4103-890d-91291aea4caa

Raisch, S., & Krakowski, S. (2021). Artificial intelligence and management: The automation–augmentation paradox. *Academy of Management Review*, 46(1), 192–210.

Rhee, J. (2023). From ELIZA to Alexa: Automated care labour and the otherwise of radical care. In J. Browne, S. Cave, E. Drage, & K. McInerney (Eds.), *Feminist AI: Critical Perspectives on Algorithms, Data, and Intelligent Machines* (pp. 155–173). Oxford: Oxford University Press.

Riley, T. (2018, 13 March). Get ready, this year your next job interview may be with an A.I. robot. *CNBC*. Retrieved from www.cnbc.com/2018/03/13/ai-job-recruiting-tools-offered-by-hirevue-mya-other-start-ups.html

Ritter, C. S. (2022). Rethinking digital ethnography: A qualitative approach to understanding interfaces. *Qualitative Research*, 22(6), 916–932.

Robertson, B. J. (2015). *Holacracy: The New Management System for a Rapidly Changing World*. New York: Henry Holt and Company.

Roose, K. (2022, 5 December). The brilliance and weirdness of ChatGPT. *The New York Times*. Retrieved from www.nytimes.com/2022/12/05/technology/chatgpt-ai-twitter.html

Russell, S., & Norvig, P. (2021). *Artificial Intelligence: A Modern Approach* (4th ed.). Harlow: Pearson.

Rzepka, D. (2023, 29 June). Grindr gibt HIV-Status seiner Nutzer weiter. *ZDF Heute*. Retrieved from www.zdf.de/nachrichten/digitales/grindr-datensch utz-hiv-status-nutzer-weitergabe-dritte-100.html

Sánchez-Monedero, J., & Dencik, L. (2019). *The Datafication of the Workplace*. Working paper, Cardiff University. Retrieved from https://datajusticeproject.net/wp-content/uploads/sites/30/2019/05/Report-The-datafication-of-the-workplace.pdf

Sánchez-Monedero, J., Dencik, L., & Edwards, L. (2020). What does it mean to "solve" the problem of discrimination in hiring? Social, technical and legal perspectives from the UK on automated hiring systems. In *Proceedings of the 2020 Conference on Fairness, Accountability, and Transparency* (pp. 458–468). New York: ACM.

Saygin, A. P., Cicekli, I., & Akman, V. (2000). Turing test: 50 years later. *Minds and Machines, 10*(4), 463–518.

Schlogl, L., Weiss, E., & Prainsack, B. (2021). Constructing the "future of work": An analysis of the policy discourse. *New Technology, Work and Employment, 36*(3), 307–326.

Schwab, K. (2018). *Shaping the Future of the Fourth Industrial Revolution*. London: Penguin Random House.

Sennett, R. (1998). *The Corrosion of Character: The Personal Consequences of Work in the New Capitalism*. New York: Norton.

Sennett, R. (2008). *The Craftsman*. London: Allen Lane.

Serenko, A. (2022). The Great Resignation: The great knowledge exodus or the onset of the Great Knowledge Revolution? *Journal of Knowledge Management, 27*(4), 1042–1055.

Shah, H., & Warwick, K. (2016). Imitating gender as a measure for artificial intelligence: Is it necessary? In *Proceedings of the 8th International Conference on Agents and Artificial Intelligence*, Vol. 1 (pp. 126–131). Setúbal: SciTePress.

Smith, A. (2021, 16 February). How to accommodate "gender-nonbinary" individuals: Neither men nor women. *SHRM* [website]. Retrieved from www.shrm.org/topics-tools/employment-law-compliance/how-to-accommodate-gender-nonbinary-individuals-neither-men-nor-women

Sparkes, A. C. (2003). Bodies, identities, selves: Autoethnographic fragments and reflections. In J. Denison, & P. Markula (Eds.), *Moving Writing: Crafting Movement in Sport Research* (pp. 51–76). New York: Peter Lang.

Spivak, G. C. (1988). Can the subaltern speak? Marxism and the interpretation of culture. In C. Nelson, & L. Grossberg (Eds.), *Marxism and the Interpretation of Culture* (pp. 271–306). Basingstoke: Macmillan.

Standage, T. (2002). *The Turk: The Life and Times of the Famous Eighteenth-Century Chess-Playing Machine*. New York: Walker Publishing.

Stephens, E. (2023). The mechanical Turk: A short history of "artificial artificial intelligence". *Cultural Studies, 37*(1), 65–87.

Strengers, Y., & Kennedy, J. (2020). *The Smart Wife: Why Siri, Alexa, and Other Smart Home Devices Need a Feminist Reboot*. Cambridge, MA: MIT Press.

Suchman, L. (2002). Located accountabilities in technology production. *Scandinavian Journal of Information Systems, 14*(2), art. 7.

Susskind, D. (2020). *A World Without Work: Technology, Automation and How We Should Respond*. London: Penguin.

Sutko, D. M. (2020). Theorizing femininity in artificial intelligence: A framework for undoing technology's gender troubles. *Cultural Studies, 34*(4), 567–592.

Sweeney, L. (2013). *Discrimination in online ad delivery*. Research paper, Harvard University. Retrieved from www.ssrn.com/abstract=2208240

Tambe, P., Cappelli, P., & Yakubovich, V. (2019). Artificial intelligence in human resources management: Challenges and a path forward. *California Management Review, 61*(4), 15–42.

The Economist (2018, 21 June). How an algorithm may decide your career. *The Economist*. Retrieved from www.economist.com/business/2018/06/21/how-an-algorithm-may-decide-your-career

Tippins, N. T. (2015). Technology and assessment in selection. *Annual Review of Organizational Psychology and Organizational Behavior, 2*(1), 551–582.

Tippins, N. T., Oswald, F. L., & McPhail, S. M. (2021). Scientific, legal, and ethical concerns about AI-based personnel selection tools: A call to action. *Personnel Assessment and Decisions, 7*(2), art. 1.

Tomasev, N., McKee, K. R., Kay, J., & Mohamed, S. (2021). Fairness for unobserved characteristics: Insights from technological impacts on queer communities. In *Proceedings of the 2021 AAAI/ACM Conference on AI, Ethics, and Society (AIES '21)* (pp. 254–265). New York: ACM.

Toupin, S. (2023). Shaping feminist artificial intelligence. *New Media & Society, 26*(1), 580–595.

Treusch, P. (2017). Re-reading ELIZA: Human–machine interaction as cognitive sense-ability. *Australian Feminist Studies, 32*(94), 411–426.

Turing, A. M. (1950). Computing machinery and intelligence. *Mind, 59*(236), 433–460.

Twine, F. W. (2022). *Geek Girls: Inequality and Opportunity in Silicon Valley*. New York: New York University Press.

Urry, J. (2016). *What Is the Future?* Cambridge: Polity.

Vassilopoulou, J., Kyriakidou, O., Özbilgin, M. F., & Groutsis, D. (2024). Scientism as illusio in HR algorithms: Towards a framework for algorithmic hygiene for bias proofing. *Human Resource Management Journal*, 34(2), 311–325.

Vincent, J. (2016, 24 March). Twitter taught Microsoft's AI chatbot to be a racist asshole in less than a day. *The Verge*. Retrieved from www.theverge.com/2016/3/24/11297050/tay-microsoft-chatbot-racist

Wachter, S. (2020). Affinity profiling and discrimination by association in online behavioural advertising. *Berkeley Technology Law Journal*, 35(2), 367–430.

Wajcman, J. (1991). *Feminism Confronts Technology*. Cambridge: Polity.

Wajcman, J. (2004). *TechnoFeminism*. Cambridge: Polity.

Wajcman, J. (2015). *Pressed for Time: The Acceleration of Life in Digital Capitalism*. Chicago, IL: University of Chicago Press.

Wajcman, J. (2017). Automation: Is it really different this time? *The British Journal of Sociology*, 68(1), 119–127.

Wajcman, J. (2019). How Silicon Valley sets time. *New Media & Society*, 21(6), 1272–1289.

Walsh, J. (2012). Not worth the sacrifice? Women's aspirations and career progression in law firms. *Gender, Work & Organization*, 19(5), 508–531.

West, C., & Zimmerman, D. H. (1987). Doing gender. *Gender & Society*, 1(2), 125–151.

West, D. M. (2018). *The Future of Work: Robots, AI, and Automation*. Washington, DC: The Brookings Institution.

Weyerer, J. C., & Langer, P. F. (2019). Garbage in, garbage out. In Y.-C. Chen, F. Salem, & A. Zuiderwijk (Eds.), *Proceedings of the 20th Annual International Conference on Digital Government Research* (pp. 509–511). New York: ACM.

Widder, D. G., & Nafus, D. (2023). Dislocated accountabilities in the "AI supply chain": Modularity and developers' notions of responsibility. *Big Data & Society*, 10(1). https://doi.org/10.1177/20539517231177620

Wilson, E. A. (2010). *Affect and Artificial Intelligence*. Seattle, WA: University of Washington Press.

Winner, L. (1980). Do artefacts have politics? *Daedalus*, 109(1), 121–136.

Wood, D., Bruner, J. S., & Ross, G. (1976). The role of tutoring in problem solving. *Journal of Child Psychology and Psychiatry*, 17(2), 89–100.

Woodfield, R. (2000). *Women, Work and Computing*. Cambridge: Cambridge University Press.

World Economic Forum (2020). *The Future of Jobs Report 2020*. Geneva: World Economic Forum. Retrieved from www.weforum.org/reports/the-future-of-jobs-report-2020

World Health Organization (2023, 5 May). Statement on the fifteenth meeting of the IHR (2005) Emergency Committee on the COVID-19 pandemic. *World Health Organization* [website]. Retrieved from https://rb.gy/9jvs2e

Young, E., Wajcman, J., & Sprejer, L. (2021). *Where Are the Women? Mapping the Gender Job Gap in AI*. London: The Alan Turing Institute.

Young, E., Wajcman, J., & Sprejer, L. (2023). Mind the gender gap: Inequalities in the emergent professions of artificial intelligence (AI) and data science. *New Technology, Work and Employment, 38*(3), 391–414.

INDEX

Note: Endnotes consist of the page number followed by "n" and the endnote number e.g., 121n1 refers to endnote 1 on page 121. The acronyms "AI" and "VR" are used in place of "artificial intelligence" and "virtual reality" respectively.

Printed and bound by CPI Group (UK) Ltd, Croydon, CR0 4YY

19/11/2024

01791331-0006